HE WIPED AWAY MY TEARS

By

Edwina Patterson

He Wiped Away My Tears

©2001 by A Heart for the Home Ministry
ISBN 1-892912-13-9
Printed in the U.S.A.

All Scripture quotations are from the King James Version of the Bible.

Cover Design: Keith Yates
Formatting: Craig Berry
Editor: Kristan Zeilan
Proofreading: Sue Pille, Melodie Blakemore, Ann Huffines, Toni Stevens, David and Donna Rizos

Requests for information or to order additional books, contact:
A Heart for the Home Ministry
3101 Deep Valley Trail
Plano, Texas 75075
1-800-344-8022
www.heart-for-home.org

This book is lovingly dedicated to
my friends
who continue to struggle with the bonds that hold them.

It is my prayer that you'll meet Jesus,
as did Mary Magdalene,
and He'll *wipe away your tears.*

HE WIPED AWAY MY TEARS

Uncertainty and pain fill my heart.
I long for the day to have a fresh start.
The tears flow freely from my eyes.
I know I must not believe the enemy's lies.

Responsibilities threaten to distract me.
Fatigue and schedules hide the Truth from me.
Time alone with Jesus is fleeting, difficult, and hard.
I seem to take for granted that He is my Lord.

I have a choice, you see,
To stay in bondage or to be set free.
No longer does Satan have a hold on me
For his control was broken on the Cross of Calvary.

My sins nailed Jesus to that tree.
His life given to pay my penalty.
When I think of all He's done for me,
I regret treating His gift so casually.

The days may be long and dreary.
Doubt may cause me to be weary.
But I have a Champion up on high,
Who comes to my rescue when I cry.

Broken dreams and bruised feelings,
Skinned knees and needed healings
Can all be placed at His feet
When with Him I choose to meet.

Tears of sorrow, pain, and shame.
Tears of joy that I can call on His name!
Tears gathered and held in a vase,
Waiting till we see each other face to face.

Until then ...
He tenderly cradles me in His arms
Shielding me from all worldly harm.
His love surrounds me, soothing my fears
... and He gently wipes away my tears.

Edwina Patterson

TABLE OF CONTENTS

INTRODUCTION

Wrapping my arms around my friend, I handed her a tissue to dry her tears. Mascara smudged her eyes and pain darkened her heart. I searched for the right words to comfort her. I knew, at this time, merely telling her God loved her and encouraging her to have patience wouldn't console her wounded spirit. And it wouldn't lift her spirits to be reminded that she wasn't the only one experiencing this same kind of pain, these feelings of discouragement, inadequacy, and doubt in her Christian life. Silently, I prayed for direction and discernment.

I began to share my testimony, my trials and struggles, of learning to *daily* live the transformed life. We cried and laughed together as I told her of my experiences. Over and over, I emphasized that transformation doesn't happen immediately. It's a process. The Lord brought to my mind the butterfly and its struggle to be free of the cocoon holding it in darkness.

There are many obstacles to metamorphosis. The tiny caterpillar is susceptible to predators and disease during the larval stage. Fungi during the spring rainfall, unstable temperatures, chemicals, and destroyed food sources affect the transformation process. The difficulties in developing from the caterpillar to the cocoon stage and the ensuing struggles to emerge from the cocoon are necessary to give the butterfly strength and beauty in its wings. *Each step has a purpose.*

Not only does the caterpillar have to guard against birds, wasps, frogs, lizards, spiders, and rodents, but a mature butterfly must also deal with pesticides, spiders, and birds. Danger lurks under leaves and on branches, waiting to hinder or devour the fragile butterfly.

Yet in His divine wisdom, God equipped certain butterflies with special protective measures. Some caterpillars—and the resulting butterflies—are able to safely ingest the poisonous qualities from their food and thus become poisonous to birds. Others wear natural disguises. Their colorings blend in with their surroundings while a few "grow" orange or red horns and spray smelly oil when threatened.

While we marvel at the ultimate beauty of a butterfly, the process of metamorphosis is painstaking and requires patience.

I reminded my friend, that although she had trusted Christ as her personal Savior years ago, her transformation into a mature Christian wasn't complete. I suggested that perhaps she was stalled in the cocoon stage struggling with issues that held her captive. Anger, resentment, unforgiveness, doubt, fear, worry, and feelings of inadequacy bind us as tightly in our Christian life as the cocoon does the butterfly.

Satan, the predator, would love to keep us in this bondage, devouring our peace, joy, and witness.

As we continued to talk, I shared the example of Mary Magdalene and the transformation that must have taken place in her life. She went from a hopeless victim to a victorious witness for the Lord. I found myself sharing the principles in this book, hoping they would encourage her.

It's my prayer that you'll be encouraged, as well.

That you'll break free of the bonds holding you in captivity.

That you'll meet each day with the joy and anticipation of serving Him.

And that *He'll wipe away your tears.*

1

MEETING HIM

---

*But we all, with open face beholding as in a glass the
glory of the Lord, are changed into the same image
from glory to glory even as by the Spirit of the Lord.*

2 Corinthians 3:18

The room was dark and cold. The lone figure huddled in the corner, shivered as if suffering from the cold. A sound startled her. She shuddered and was immediately on her feet. Her eyes, swollen from lack of sleep and constant weeping, quickly surveyed her surroundings. Fear seemed to emulate from every inch of the room. Anguished, she pulled her fingers through her matted hair.

Turning around, confused, she searched the room until the terror engulfed her, and she ran from it oblivious to the furniture in her way. Fresh bruises and welts added their presence to the black and blue ones already visible.

She stumbled from the house. The sunlight was far too bright for her sensitive eyes. As if to protect, she covered them and ran headlong through the crowd now used to her frequent outbursts of panic. No longer was she greeted with laughter and jeers, people simply chose to ignore her. With disdain, men and women moved out of her way. Mothers protectively placed their arms around their young children, shielding them from her touch.

She fell and then struggled to her feet. Overlooking her skinned knees and stumped toes, she continued to race on. The sharp stones in the path didn't faze her.

Nothing seemed real anymore.

Her life was spinning out of control.

Pain was her constant companion.

Finally reaching the outskirts of the city, she collapsed at the foot of a tree. Leaning her head back against the rough bark, she wondered if this torture would ever end. The tears flowed freely. If she could just rest awhile, but sleep eluded her. Neither day nor night afforded her rest, her mind was constantly tormented. She couldn't cry out for help, so she suffered *in silence.*

She was jolted from her thoughts by the noise of a crowd.

Had they followed her?

She quickly crouched behind the tree, using it as a shield. Warily, she peaked around the trunk and noticed men, women, and children hurrying down the road, completely unaware of her hiding place. Relieved they weren't searching for her, but curious about their excitement and destination, she overcame the battle within her and followed. Always ready to screen herself from their view, she carefully sneaked closer and closer.

Suddenly, the crowd stopped, surrounded Someone, and spilled over onto the grassy meadow. Voices were raised, not in anger or fear, but to gain the attention of one Man. His answers and comments seemed to pacify them. Amazed, she noticed the throng of people being seated in orderly groups, ready to hear more. The Man sat in their midst and patiently responded to their questions.

She heard some of the people refer to Him as "Teacher," while others called Him "Jesus." From their comments, she learned he was capable of performing miracles. Excitedly, those around her discussed His healing the blind and lame. Part of her sneered and ridiculed their claims. Another part knew exactly who He was. A tiny, little part wondered, "If He could heal a leper, could He free me from the torment and pain I experience?" She stood still, lost and bewildered.

She became indignant and defiant when He professed to forgive sins. Something inside her wanted to lash out at such sayings, but the words remained silent, caught in her throat.

Absorbed in the moment, she didn't notice the hush settling over the people.

The silence finally grabbed her attention.

Frightened, she realized everyone was staring at her!

Should she run away?

Fresh tears streamed down her cheeks, and she quickly turned to flee.

Then ...He said her name, "Mary."

She hesitated. Surely, He didn't mean *her*? How could He know *her* name?

But again, clearly and with authority, He said, "Mary."

With fear and trembling, she stopped. She was afraid to disobey His voice.

Blinded by her tears, she reluctantly turned to face Him. He directed her to come to Him. Each step seemed to take an eternity as she slowly approached Him. Her mind screamed rebellion, panic, dread, alarm. Yet something in her heart pulled her closer. Through her tears, she noticed His eyes. They drew her with cords of love, as a magnet will draw metal toward it. Now oblivious to the crowd, she steadily moved forward, for she only had eyes for Him.

Standing before Him, she heard Him say she was free, that *all* her chains were broken. He said she no longer had to be afraid or tormented. The chains of fear, doubt, anger, humiliation, and panic were destroyed.

<u>*All*</u> *her chains were broken.* With power, He proclaimed that her bondage to the slave market of sin was rent. Her shackles, her fetters were removed. She was free!

Then He gently wiped away her tears.

The multitude watched in stunned amazement to see Mary, the anguished demoniac, now filled with peace. The agitation, despair, anger, bitterness, horror, confusion, and discouragement were gone. For the first time in years, she felt tranquil. *Her tears were gone!* She felt like dancing!

With inexplicable joy, she skipped from the group. Indeed, her chains had been broken—she'd been cleansed! She began to clap her hands and noticed how dirty they were. Then she realized her clothes were muddy and torn, and her hair was filthy. She rushed home and, to the astonishment of her parents, bathed from head to toe. Her once dingy hair now shined brightly with golden red highlights. Her old clothes were burned, and fresh ones were made ready for her.

Scrubbing her body, she silently thanked God for cleansing her from angry outbursts, cruel words, defiance toward her parents, savage jealousy, and for causing so much heartache to those around her. These sins were forgiven and no longer belonged in her.

When she finally emerged, she not only looked like a different person, she *was* a new creation! Her demeanor was calm and thoughtful. Her rediscovered smile was genuine. Laughter bubbled up within her and randomly burst forth. Her eyes no longer glistened with tears, but with joy. Those around her marveled at her newfound peace and happiness.

What had happened to her?

As she smoothed the folds of her skirt, she wondered at the radical change in her life. What had He done to her? She had been a child of wrath, a child of disobedience, experienced no hope in her life, and walked according to the prince of the power of the air (Ephesians 2:2,3,12). Mary had been held captive by Satan. Now the wretchedness was gone, the condemnation was nullified. With just a few simple words, the Teacher had freed her from the bondage and torment controlling her. She was not her former self. She was different, radically changed.

Her circumstances hadn't changed.

She had changed!

And she longed to understand what had occurred. She had to find Jesus and discover the truth.

&* I suppose it could have happened that way. &*

As I've poured over manuscripts and books regarding Mary Magdalene, I can just imagine the events unfolding as I've suggested. My heart is drawn to Mary, for in her I see an example of a transformed life. How could a woman who was so tormented, angry, hopeless, and controlled by demons courageously stand at the foot of the cross and be singled out to be the first to see the resurrected Lord? I set out to discover as much about her as I could. How was she changed? When was she changed? What were the steps in her transformation? Was there something I could learn from her?

We don't know when or where Jesus met Mary of Magdala initially, but she does appear in all four gospels. Neither does the Bible supply us with the specifics of Mary's divine physical and spiritual healing. Scripture simply states Jesus healed her of seven demons (Luke 8:2; Mark 16:9). Since demon possession during biblical days was associated with both physical and moral-spiritual illness, the reference to "seven demons" probably emphasizes either the gravity of her condition or the recurrent nature of it.

My studies revealed that Mary of Magdala was one of the most prominent of the Galilean women who followed Jesus. Most likely the city of Magdala was a happy place in Mary's childhood. It stood on the shore of the Sea of Galilee. In Roman times it was a small fishing and shipbuilding city. It held a hippodrome for horse and chariot races and had a reputation as a city of the "fast life".

It is believed that her family was a part of the small Jewish settlement in the predominantly Gentile city (their synagogue was approximately 27 feet by 24 feet, indicating an insignificant Jewish population). History suggests that, like most Jewish children, Mary grew up hearing the Law, listening to the marvels wrought by God in Egypt, in the desert, and in the promised land, and joining her family in celebrating Israel's feasts.

She is not to be confused with Mary of Bethany (John 11:1-12:8; Luke 10:38-42), and there is no historical evidence to identify her with the harlot in Luke 7:36-50. In fact, not a word is said against her personal character. Perhaps the unsavory reputation of the city of Magdala may have helped cast suspicion on her character. Not only was it a city recognized for its wealth, but also for it licentiousness, much as Corinth and Sodom and Gomorrah were known.

The specifics of when the evil spirits entered Mary and how they controlled her are not included in the Scriptures. They are left to our imagination, but we may gather much information from the record of other similar cases.

I believe Mary Magdalene represents those who for years
have experienced great heartbreak,
been heavily burdened with discouragement,
bound with cords of doubt,
subject to torment,
endured uncontrollable fits of anger,
and suffered deep despondency.
She depicts those who have come under the distracting and depressing power of Satan. They are prisoners in cells of

sorrow held by chains of hopelessness. They are the pictures of wretchedness, agony, and misery.

Today we would consider Mary Magdalene to be demented, a completely helpless individual controlled by seasons of depression. Had she suffered from some form of physical disease, help might have been attainable. But man could do nothing for her.

Surgery couldn't help her.

No drugs could lull her into peaceful sleep.

Probably those who knew her thought death would be a relief to her and would also relieve her family of worry, anxiety, and fear. Imagine their sorrow as they helplessly watched her endure an agony they couldn't alleviate.

I wonder how many of you today, or perhaps a loved one, are in the same condition now? Are you bound with invisible chains, experiencing temporary seasons of frightful depression, enduring the horror of darkness and doubt, and held tight with the cords of discouragement? Maybe you feel caught in a vicious cycle. You're overwhelmed with responsibilities, burdened with feelings of inadequacy and fear, and you too, have no peace in your life.

Can you identify with Mary Magdalene?

Are your nights spent restlessly tossing and turning, haunted by the events of the day?

Are your days a whirlwind of activities as you try to balance schedules, agendas, and family?

Do you sometimes feel you are treading water, barely able to keep your head above the surface?

Is *peace* a foreign word in your vocabulary?

If you're honest with yourself and answered, "Yes" to any of the above questions, you're not alone. In fact, you are among the majority in the world today, embarrassed to admit their problems and silent battles—oppressed by feelings of isolation, depression, and inadequacy. Restlessness, fear, confusion, and discouragement can be binding chains rendering you powerless, ineffective, and...*reduced to tears.*

You may be a member of a church and even profess to be a Christian. After all, your parents went to church every Sunday, and America is *supposed* to be a Christian nation. Surely, you can become a Christian by osmosis, you mistakenly believe. And you muddle along on your own, wondering why your life is in such chaos.

The case of Mary Magdalene is common to all the unconverted, those who don't know Jesus as Savior.

Perhaps you've never met Jesus.

At the same time, consider that Mary was especially exposed to Satanic attack. Magdala lay among the cities nearest the Gadarenes, the central haunt of unchained demons. Therefore, Mary was particularly in peril of Satanic interference, as were all those living in that area. Lusts of the flesh, desires of the mind, pride, and a stubborn refusal to yield herself to the promptings of the Holy Spirit may have opened her soul to the Evil One (1 Samuel 16:14). (Could this be a description of America today?)

Maybe you've given your heart to Jesus, but you've never developed an intimate relationship with Him and haven't experienced the power of a transformed life. Unconsciously, you too, have been subjected to Satanic interferences. Constant exposure to lack of morals, filthy language, and violence pollute and profane our minds. Most of today's music, entertainment, magazines, and television are simply channels Satan uses to fill our minds and our homes with seduction, rebellion, and violence. We've become desensitized to his evil methods and fall prey to his control.

Often we give up and resolve to remain in despair, believing we cannot break free.

What a lie!

The father of lies, Satan, would love to keep you in bondage, chained to darkness, weeping. Mary couldn't drive the demons out. But Jesus cast them out because of who He is, the Sinless Son of All Powerful God! Christ alone has the power to break the chains that bind you.

Only He can *wipe away your tears.*

✝

Whatever the process, the fact is, evil spirits entered Mary and held her captive—a helpless victim (Acts 10:38).

Her human heart was turned into temporary hell.

Either someone brought Mary to Jesus or, in one of her rampages, she caught His attention. And He took notice of her need. His sensitive eyes looked past the dirt and grime on her clothing and body, past the sin spoiling her, and saw the needs of her heart ... *just as He does with you and me.*

There's hope, precious one. Even if your heartaches have shut you up, they cannot shut Him out!

His eyes can penetrate the very depths of your soul.

Praise God, though a legion of demons encompasses your heart, the power of Jesus is able to cast them out and set you free (Psalm 107:20; 105:20; Matthew 8:16, 12:28; Luke 4:36, 11:20). No matter how removed you are from God, His arms are open to you, waiting for you. He desires to encase you in His love and heal you by His grace.

Mary was healed immediately! The Lord ransomed her from the hand of the enemy. It simply took a word from

Jesus, and poor demonic Mary was filled with peace. We may safely conclude that her soul's deliverance from the seven demons was simultaneous with her heart's conversion to God. Many times the cure of bodily ailments by Christ was accompanied by the healing of the soul, and the outward health became the witness of the new life within (Mark 2:10-11).

She went from the depths of mental distress to the heights of spiritual joy.

And she longed to know more!

Do you suffer with feelings of anxiety and hopelessness?

I wonder, precious one, if you have discovered the truth Mary learned?

Perhaps depression, anger, and fear are not the chains that hold you. You may feel pretty good about yourself. Maybe you volunteer at the local hospital, lead a Cub Scout troop, teach a children's Sunday School class, or sing in the church choir. You may boast that no one can point out a single, overt sin in your life. Yet, that in itself is a most detestable sin—the sin of pride—pride of your own goodness. And sin, no matter how insignificant you may deem it, holds you in a prison, locking you away from God's blessings.

In God's eyes, there are no big sins or little sins. Anything that does not please God is sin. Neglecting your family, constant complaining, and worry are all sins to God. Sin is falling short of something—falling short of the glory of God (Romans 3:23).

There is only one solution to the sin problem in your life—Jesus Christ! The Bible makes it very clear that we are set free by God's grace through faith in the Lord Jesus. It doesn't matter who you are or how bad or good you may think you are. In order to experience God's precious salvation and freedom from the chains that hold you, you must be cleansed just like everyone else—by placing your trust in Christ (John 1:12).

> Christ longs to remove your heart of stone,
>   cleanse your conscience,
>   cast out Satan,
>   break your chains,
>   and *wipe away your tears.*

Many people say they believe the Bible and what it says about Christ, but they've never personally received the freedom that comes from yielding their lives to Jesus. The world is full of the refined, and the religious, *but lost*; full of those zealous for the traditions of churches, blameless, *but still lost.* Our best efforts and our most noble ambitions, if offered as an excuse or a substitute for faith in Christ, are unacceptable to God.

Simply going to church is no substitute for a relationship with Jesus Christ. Singing in the choir, volunteering at a homeless shelter, going on mission trips, and serving on church committees without knowing and trusting Christ as your personal Savior are unacceptable to God. Your only hope is to admit your sin, ask for God's mercy, and receive His forgiveness (Proverbs 28:13). Christ stands ready to overthrow the father of lies in your life.

He's done it before— for Mary Magdalene.

He can do it for you and me!

Oh precious friend, if you haven't met Jesus, it's my prayer that you'll no longer be taken in by Satan's lies. Don't hesitate another minute. Pray something like this,

"Lord Jesus, I admit I'm a sinner. I acknowledge I cannot help myself. I believe You are the Son of God ,that You became a man, lived a sinless life, and died on the cross for my sin. I believe You arose from the dead. Forgive me for my wrong choices and sinful habits. I desire the blessing of Your daily presence. I choose to trust in You. In Jesus' name, Amen."

Perhaps in the past you've given your heart to Jesus, but you haven't yielded every area of your life into His control. You wonder why you are constantly dealing with anger, depression, discouragement, and hopelessness. It's my prayer that you'll pause right now and surrender every nook and cranny of your life to Him. Hold nothing back! Perhaps you'd like to pray:

> *"Lord Jesus, I give myself to You, nothing held back. No longer will I try to control my home, family, occupation, finances, or recreation. From now on, I yield to You, trusting You to do what is best for me. You be in charge... and may I listen to You In Jesus' name, Amen."*

If you prayed either of these suggested prayers and really meant it, your chains have been broken!

You are now free.

The transformation begins and...

He'll gently *wipe away your tears.*

2

FALLING IN LOVE

That Christ may dwell in your hearts by faith; that ye, being rooted and grounded in love, may be able to comprehend with all saints what is the breadth, and length, and depth, and height; and to know the love of Christ, which passeth knowledge, that ye might be filled with all the fullness of God.

Ephesians 3:17-19

By the light of the little oil lamp, Mary carefully packed a few things. She glanced around the room...so many memories. Those of her childhood were pleasant, but those from the recent years were painful. Yet, at the same time, those bitter remembrances were replaced with the sweet knowledge of her freedom.

A peace that passed all understanding now filled her soul.

Lovingly, she stroked the hair of her younger sister, praying that she, too, would soon come to know Jesus. Tiptoeing from the room, she met her mother and father on their way to the kitchen. Together they prepared a lunch for Mary, carefully wrapping it in a cloth. Their daughter was healed and home again. Reluctantly, but with much love, they tried to understand her desire to leave their care and follow the Teacher. Grateful to Him for her healing, they relinquished their responsibility for her, and with trepidation, gave her their blessing.

Tightly embracing her parents and reminding them how much she loved them, Mary turned and joined the little group of women who traveled from town to town ministering to the needs of the Teacher and His followers. Her parents took comfort in knowing the women she accompanied were matrons of established reputation. It was customary for Jewish matrons or widows to travel with noted teachers of the law, to benefit from their instructions, and to supply their wants. Joanna, the wife of Herod's steward, promised to take Mary under her wing and introduce her to the tasks before her. They prepared meals, set up camp, and tended to the general needs of the group following Him.

As Mary walked along, she marveled at the beauty of the Sea of Galilee and the surrounding mountains, which just the day before had been filled with fearful, haunting forms. But the metamorphosis had begun. Now the brilliance of the sun, the lush, green earth, the blue sky, and the majesty of the hills brought joy and happiness into her life. She saw them through new eyes. The scales blinding her sight had been removed.

What a name to her is the name of Jesus now!

Savior, Redeemer, Deliverer.

The sweetest name on earth!

Jesus of Nazareth had freed Mary from her torment, redeemed her soul, and rescued the hopeless captive that she was.

As the women worked and visited together, Mary constantly questioned them. Finally Joanna and Susanna threw their arms in the air and laughingly told her they were exhausted from answering so many questions. They compared her to a two-year-old who continued to ask "Why." But Mary ignored their good-natured teasing because she longed to know much more. Shaking their heads, the women patiently shared with her all they had learned while serving Jesus.

As she helped Joanna bake the matzo for the evening meal, she heard that she was God's treasured possession (Exodus 19:5), He would comfort her in all her troubles (2 Corinthians 1:3-4), and He was her provider and would meet all of her needs (Matthew 6:31-33). Although she was having difficulty processing all the information, she didn't want the women to stop sharing with her. Almost in popcorn style, they would call out truths they had learned.

God will never stop doing good to us (Jeremiah 32:40).

We are not to be afraid, for God is with us (Isaiah 41:10).

As a shepherd carries a lamb, God carries us close to His heart (Isaiah 40:11).

When we are brokenhearted, He is close to us (Psalm 34:18).

He is our Father, and He loves us even as He loves His son, Jesus (John 17:23).

In Jesus, His love for us is revealed (John 17:26).

We are to forgive others as God forgives us (Matthew 6:14-15).

We are to love one another as God loves us (John 13:34).

And He loved us with an everlasting love (Jeremiah 31:3; John 13:1; John 3:16)!

Slowly, Mary began to gain a small inkling of God's great, unconditional love.

It was a love that had compassion, saw her true needs, and healed her. It was love that disregarded her pitiful state and saw in her a creature worth redeeming. It was love that reached out to the lame, blind, hungry, weary, and disheartened.

It was love in action.

Mary learned that love is not simply a word. It is so much more. It's something very real that can be seen and experienced. Even though she couldn't comprehend the full meaning of God's love, she responded to it. She *chose* to follow Him.

> She gave her whole heart,
>   her whole means,
>   and her whole time
>   to the One who had set her free
>   and *wiped away her tears*.

❧ *Perhaps it happened that way.* ❧

Scripture doesn't elaborate on the spiritual growth process of Mary, but I envision she gleaned information about the Lord every way she could. I believe she hungered to know all about Jesus and His teachings. Not only did Mary listen to the older women around her, I think she also interviewed His apostles and the crowds following Him. A little here, a little there. Much as a detective pieces a puzzle together, Mary diligently persisted.

As I studied her life, I can't conceive that laughter or teasing caused Mary not to persevere in her quest for knowledge about Jesus. He had redeemed her, broken her chains, and filled her life with peace. I think her desire to gain information and understanding about Him could be compared to a child eagerly looking forward to Christmas morning. Nothing deters or distracts him...neither could anything hinder Mary!

I imagine her struggles could be compared to a butterfly slowly emerging from a cocoon. The vigorous effort necessary to break free from the tightly encased covering is used to make the butterfly strong and give its wings their brilliant colors. In the journey to develop a transformed life, battles and grasping for knowledge are necessary for building faith in Jesus.

Mary's head introduced her to the truth.

Now her heart appropriated the truth.

Her desires, choices, motives, decisions, and actions demonstrated Who was in control of her life. His love flowing through her became a spontaneous response from her heart, spilling out on those around her.

She fell in love with the Lover of her soul!

Most people in the world today know the words "Jesus loves me, this I know." But they have no understanding of God's love. They simply repeat words they were exposed to as children. They experience a society full of hatred, anger, and violence. Therefore, it's understandable that the concept of God's unconditional love is foreign to them.

Agape love, the kind of love that springs from within the heart of a person without regard to the worthiness of its love object, is a description of God's unconditional love. He proved His love for us in while we were yet sinners, Christ died for us. We didn't deserve God's love Gift, but He willingly gave His Only Son so we could have a love relationship with Him (John 3:16).

When we evidence *agape* love in our lives, we love others like God loves us. As an expression of love toward the Lord, we are to manifest the same love toward others. Our attitudes, actions, and responses must seek their welfare and good, whether we believe they are deserving or lovable. This love is totally unselfish. Sounds impossible, doesn't it? It *is* impossible for us to possess *agape* love *unless* we know Jesus.

Mary and I both discovered the principle of *agape* love meant that every believer's conduct should be controlled by the love of Christ. Everything we do, everything we say, our every motive should be to please Him. And that scared me to death. I wondered how I would ever be able to measure up.

Slowly, I learned it doesn't usually happen all at once, but our devotion to the Savior will deepen as we increasingly understand the greatness of Christ's love for us.

I came to understand that God's love is expressed by sincerity in our lives. The believer motivated by the love of Christ is sincere, hates evil, and loves righteousness. Genuineness doesn't wear a mask. Our love for others is honest, not selfish or self-serving. When we demonstrate an outward show of love, but actually harbor ill will and hatred in our hearts, we are hypocrites (Romans 12:9), and bring shame to His name.

Another mark of Christian love is an affectionate regard for others (Romans 12:10). Self-centered, "me-first" attitudes of jealousy and envy are set aside when friends receive promotions and recognition. Transformed lives are to exhibit warmth, happiness, and selflessness toward other believers. We are to express joy when other children of God succeed, give unselfish help to those in need, and always encourage and support others as they mature spiritually. Words like, "I'm proud of you," "You're an example of God's love," "You're an encouragement to me," enhance a believer's spiritual journey whether they are new or mature believers.

Evidence of God's love in our lives doesn't demand large dramatic, public expressions. Rather it's seen most clearly in the gentle, constant, small examples of Christ-like living. Recently, this principle was graphically illustrated to me at a time when I was overwhelmed with a very large project. I kept telling myself, "I can do all things through Christ which strengtheneth me" (Philippians 4:13). But as I stared at boxes and boxes of newsletters, I issued a call for help. Ministry volunteers, neighbors, and our children responded.

As busy as young mothers are driving carpools to schools, dance lessons, and football practice, and keeping up with laundry and meals, I was amazed when our daughter Jayme spent countless hours folding and stuffing newsletters. Repeatedly she picked up more and more materials, rearranging her own schedule to help. Yes, she was bailing her mother out of a difficult situation, but more than that, she was expressing God's love to me. Through the years,

I've watched her quietly serving in her home, children's school, neighborhood, and church. She tirelessly shares God's love in the mission field in which He has placed her.

It only takes a moment to call a friend or write a simple note of encouragement, but the results last a lifetime. God uses our desires to express His love and blesses the recipient. Many days when I've been overwhelmed and tired, a note comes in the mail or a message is left on the recorder. All of a sudden I'm no longer weary. I've been recharged. I'm encouraged and inspired to persevere. I face the day with a different outlook—looking unto Him who has promised to continue working on me until He finishes (Philippians 1:6).

The individuals whose lives and actions are compelled by God's love will also be zealous in the performance of their Christian duties (Romans 12:11). These believers will not casually respond to their obligations, but will serve the Lord with enthusiasm and fervency. Their word can be trusted. When they commit to teach a class, serve on a committee, or bring donuts for refreshments, they do it! Problems don't deter them. Difficulties don't cause them to give up in despair. Staying focused on Jesus, they continue on. They are devoted and dedicated, not easily distracted.

Diligently, they are driven by a passion to share His love—they keep on keeping on.

When the Lord nudges them and instructs them to do something, zealous believers won't hesitate, make excuses, or postpone obeying His instructions. With a heart full of love for Him, they willingly, joyfully, immediately obey. While they may not understand why, they step out in faith and obey ... whatever His call, trusting Him for guidance.

In addition, the consciousness of Christ's love will produce generosity (Romans 12:13). We will no longer be greedy or stingy with our money *or* our time. God has filled our lives with blessings, and we gladly share with others as we become aware of their needs.

A freedom manifests itself in our lives.

Materialism and luxuries do not keep us chained to covetous or resentful attitudes. When we're transformed, we willingly make sacrifices for one another, say no to ourselves, go the extra mile, and put aside all petty selfishness and pride. Preparing a meal for an ill friend becomes a gift of love, not merely a begrudged responsibility. Caring for a neighbor's children while she makes a hospital visit becomes an opportunity to wrap those children in God's love. Opening our homes for prayer or Bible study, maintaining hospital vigils, helping pay the electric bill for a needy family, and donating a church camp scholarship to a needy teenager all become evidence of His love controlling our lives.

Compassion is another characteristic of a changed heart that follows Christ. It is filled with genuine love for others (Romans 12:15). We usually think of compassion as a feeling of sorrow or pity for the sufferings or misfortunes of others. But in biblical days, the Greek word denoted both rejoicing with others in their happiness and sharing in their sadness, disappointments, or bereavement. It took sympathy a step further to an expression of sincere love— love free of pretense. We might use the term *tenderhearted* to describe the compassionate heart. God's love flows through the tenderhearted onto a hurting and unbelieving world.

How do you feel when you see suffering and sorrow?

Our society today has become calloused and hardened. The news media clearly reveals wounded people in war-torn areas, starving children in famine-stricken lands, and suffering families after a devastating flood or tornado. What do most of us do when confronted with these images? While we may express sorrow, we usually turn our backs, change the channel, and simply ignore the situations. All too often we are engrossed in our own problems and these conditions make little impression upon us.

This is not God's desire for us. He expects us to be sensitive to the plight of others, so we will be moved to sincere prayer and sacrificial giving. Deep concern for others is a vital ingredient in expressing *agape* love.

✝

A forgiving spirit also expresses godly love (Luke 6:27-28). It's easier to forgive loved ones or those who think well of us; but in a transformed life, the Lord commands us to cultivate a willingness to forgive *all* others, even when they wrong us maliciously and repeatedly. And we don't like to hear that. We prefer to nurse our grudges and grievances. We pet them and carry our believed injustices around with us as we would a favorite pet, fondly stroking them.

Christ's command to love our enemies takes away all our excuses. We can no longer say, "I can't forgive him. Look what he's done to me!"

Jesus gave us the supreme example of forgiving people who wrong us when, from the cross, He prayed for His tormentors.

If we refuse to forgive others, we live in disobedience to the Lord and prove we haven't really changed after all.

Forgiveness doesn't mean the other person is right. It means we are right with God. A refusal to obey this command has resulted in broken homes, rebellious children, and ruined lives, not to mention broken fellowship with God and the loss of real joy. It's a shame Christians who have experienced the Lord's forgiveness for a mountain of sin and guilt could begrudge forgiveness to another. Unforgiving believers are bound to be miserable Christians. They remain caught in their tight cocoons, refusing to break free.

If you are unwilling to forgive because you continue to hold on to hatred or anger in your heart, you are hurting yourself and others. You may bring depression and physical affliction upon yourself. God expects you to forgive others. Completely! Even if they have wronged you greatly and with malice. Perhaps unforgiveness was one of Mary Magdalene's problems.

If you've ever known God's agape love, you understand how it fills your heart and takes up residence in your life. If you don't know this love, you can. He's just waiting to welcome you into His arms. He longs to love you. Won't you let Him?

Perhaps you've experienced His love, but your love for Him has grown somewhat cold. If you long to revive it,

focus on His love for you. "God commendeth His love
toward us, in that, while we were yet sinners, Christ died
for us" (Romans 5:8). When we were wretched, awful,
without hope, the Lord loved us even then. Meditate on His
unselfish love. Think what a relationship with you cost
Him. Do you ever wonder if He looks down on our daily
lives and questions if it was worth it?

Jesus loves us. That's why He left His home in glory and
descended to earth to endure heartaches and pain. It was
His sympathetic love that led Him up to the cross on
Golgatha. He did it for you and me! Christ actually put
Himself in our place on the cross. He experienced what we
deserved. The Lord endured the suffering that resulted from
our sin.

Calvary was love in action.

And Christ's not satisfied with a long distance relationship
with us. He longs for a moment-by-moment love
relationship with each of us. He wants us to reach up and
take His nail-pierced hand and show evidence of His love
to an unbelieving world. If you really love Him, you won't
be able to keep His love to yourself. You'll want to share it
with others.

I remember watching our son at football practice years ago. Calisthenics, drills, plays, and endurance exercises on hot afternoons made the sessions long and wearing, especially for the offensive and defensive lines. At the beginning of practice, everyone was full of energy. The coaches' demands were easily and quickly performed, but they met with some resistance when they required the team to run wind sprints at the *close* of practice. The goal was to increase the team's stamina enabling them to perform well at the end of the game as well as at the beginning.

Those big linemen dreaded running wind sprints. They were hot, sweaty, and worn out, but there were no excuses or leniency for them. Everyone ran. As I observed our son running, I knew it was taking all his strength, not just to keep up with the others, but to stay close to the front group.

When practice was over and Russell finally came to the car, I asked him why he was playing football and how he had the stamina to keep going. Without hesitation, he replied that he'd prayed about it and believed God intended for him to play football. After all, the Lord hadn't given him the body of a soccer player. He told me he survived practice by keeping focused on Jesus Christ and what He endured for him on the cross. He said the little bit of pain he experienced during football practice was nothing compared to the crucifixion.

Then he turned to me and exclaimed that He had shared Jesus with two players that day.

Let me ask you, do you think the grueling practice was worth it?

I'll bet the angels in heaven were rejoicing over those two new believers.

Choose to make God's mercy toward you the pattern of your attitude toward others. When you do, you reap spiritual, psychological, and physical benefits. But most important, others will see God's love exhibited in your life.

And maybe, just maybe, they'll hunger to know the One you're in love with! And they'll choose to fall in beside you and follow Him, too.

I have decided to follow Jesus.
I have decided to follow Jesus.
I have decided to follow Jesus.
No turning back,
No turning back.

3

LEARNING TO BE OBEDIENT

But this thing commanded I them, saying, Obey My voice,
and I will be your God, and ye shall be My people:
and walk ye in all the ways that I have commanded you,
that it may be well unto you.

Jeremiah 7:23

The wind blowing across the Sea of Galilee brought a welcome coolness and anticipation to the campsite. The days of travel had been hot and dusty. Long hours ministering to the crowds had left the apostles and women drained. They all longed for much-needed rest. Perhaps when they reached Capernaum they could find time to relax and refresh themselves. Trying to hurry the women along, the apostles helped gather the cooking utensils and leftover food.

Mary seemed preoccupied this morning and often stopped and stared into space. The needs of the people seemed to overwhelm her and tears of sadness filled her eyes, yet her passion to see others set free strengthened her. She desired to wrap her arms around each one and tell them of God's great love. To get their attention, she was willing to stand on a rooftop to make them realize Jesus could do so much more than just heal their bodies, He could break *all* cords holding them captive.

She knew, because He'd done it for her!

With resolve, she straightened her shoulders and determined not to rest until those with hurting hearts were comforted by His love.

Joanna stood back and watched Mary. By now they were accustomed to Mary's questions and times of silent contemplation. Gently, Joanna called for her to join them as they began the day's journey. Mary fell in line with the other women and listened to their idle chatter. Talk of visiting friends, would they arrive at Capernaum before the evening meal, and where the Master would choose to go next occupied their conversation.

The women were walking so slowly Mary could hardly stand it. Jesus and the apostles were discussing something, and she wanted to hear what they were saying. Sidestepping the stragglers, Mary quickly made her way to the front of the group. Jesus noticed the movement and smiled when He saw Mary. It warmed His heart to see how hungry she was to learn. He deliberately slowed His pace and repeated Himself so she could understand the discussion.

Pointing to the birds in the air, fields of wheat, and plants beside the path, He shared parable after parable. He longed for them to understand His teachings, so He carefully used stories and word pictures to illustrate truths. Once again, He stressed the importance of obedience. Simply studying God's Word, having more faith, and offering more prayer without obedience was a shallow, empty religion. He drew their attention to the religious hypocrites of the day. They wore the Law bound to their foreheads, arms, and hems of garments, yet their lives were barren and meaningless.

A transformed life, a Father-pleasing life, is not gained by head knowledge alone. At the same time, it cannot be accomplished without knowing the Word of God. It takes a combination of head *and* heart knowledge. When the truth is written on our hearts, obedience becomes an act of love.

Jesus claimed that the same obedience He rendered to God should be evident in everyone who desired to be His disciple. He came into the world for one purpose. "I seek not mine own will, but the will of the Father which hath sent me" (John 5:30). He lived only to carry out God's will. It was the controlling power of His life. In everyday affairs, the Lord demonstrated obedience as a way of life, not just a single act now and then. It was to be the spirit of the whole life.

Mary was so absorbed in what the Teacher was saying, she didn't see the rock in the path, and she stumbled.

Quickly Peter reached over and steadied her.

Wherever he turned, Mary seemed to be there. At first it irritated Peter, but now he'd grown accustomed to her shadow. They shared a kindred spirit—impulsiveness, industrious, and a willingness to pitch in and help. Peter had come to think of her as a little sister—to put up with, look after, and protect. He gave her the once over to make sure she was all right, glared her into silence, and then turned his attention back to the Teacher.

Jesus spoke so passionately about obedience. He stressed that obedience sometimes stood for a bondage to rules, a slavery to things. He explained that true obedience springs from a heart of love yielded to the One being obeyed. With Christ, obedience was a joy (John 4:34). He hungered to please the Father. He knew it's the joy of hearing His Father's voice that provides the delight and strength of true obedience. And He longed for His followers to possess the same pleasure and contentment.

The Lord emphasized that obedience is the cornerstone to our faith in God and is the true mark of a changed life. He promised, "whosoever shall do the will of my Father which is in heaven, the same is my brother, and sister, and mother" (Matthew 12:50). He explained that obedient servants would share a family resemblance. (I wonder...who do people say you resemble? Has anyone ever mistaken you for Jesus? Do others know you are a member of His family?)

Mary struggled to digest all Jesus was teaching before she wandered off into her own thoughts. She caught the last part of the Teacher's statement, "If you love Me, you'll keep My commandments" (John 14:15-21).

> ❧ *Maybe Jesus did walk along*
> *and teach this way.* ❧

For most people, *obedience* is an uncomfortable, prickly word.

It makes us wiggle and squirm with distaste.

It conjures up pictures of evil taskmasters, authoritative parents, controlling employers, uncompromising judges, and dictatorial teachers.

We don't like the word *obedience* because it calls to our memory all the times we've been *disobedient.*

Throughout Scripture, reinforced again and again, God reveals His mind set on obedience. While the expression "obey the commandment" is seldom used in the Bible, on almost every page there is a reference to obedience. God usually says, "obey Me" or "obey (or hearken to) My voice." Therein lies the key to obedience. Our obedience is to God—not to rules or regulations! An intimate relationship with Him, desiring to please Him, and living a transformed life make obedience a joy instead of an obligation. From the very beginning, God said nothing directly about faith, humility, or love because obedience includes *all* of these things.

Noah, Abraham, Moses, Shadrach, Meshach, Abednego, Daniel, and so many more are examples of those who obeyed God's commands. Building the ark, offering Isaac at the altar, leading the Israelites in the wilderness, walking in the fiery furnace, and praying in a lion's den didn't bring anyone closer to the Lord, but their obedience and faith in God did.

It is the obedient heart that the Lord blesses with His favor and presence (Deuteronomy 11:26-28).

At the same time, included in God's Word are many instances of disobedience and its consequences. "I set before you ...a blessing, if ye obey ...and a curse, if ye will not obey" (Deuteronomy 11:26-28).

God will not honor the individual who is disobedient.

Nor does the Lord desire partial obedience.

God insists on exact, full obedience.

Today many try to change, edit, and rearrange obedience to make it easier for them. They believe many of God's commands are difficult, archaic, or not meant for them. It might *inconvenience* them to be obedient. They prefer to take their teaching from men and women rather than serve God and receive instructions directly from Him. Why? Because it's a lot easier to make excuses or say "no" to men and women than it is to God. Often we willfully treat His commands as suggestions. Scripture says, "...Because thou has rejected the word of the Lord, He hath also rejected thee" (1 Samuel 15:22-23). If we love Him, we'll obey Him.

There is no substitute for obedience.

Other times we're simply too lazy to dig into the Bible and listen for God's instructions. We'd rather someone else do the work for us. And we comfortably sit back absorbing another's ideas. When this happens, our faith stands in the wisdom of men and not in the power of God.

What then is the secret of obedience?

What makes obedience palatable?

At the moment we chose to trust Christ as our personal Savior, His righteousness cleansed us from all sin. We received righteousness even though we may have had limited knowledge of obedience. The secret to true obedience is a close and unmistakable personal relationship with God. All our attempts to be fully obedient will fail until we develop an intimate fellowship with the Lord.

When we become conscious of His holy presence in our lives, we *choose* to be obedient. Obedience then becomes the path to a full, intimate relationship with God ... and to developing a transformed life.

We cannot slip casually into obedience. First of all, it takes self-examination, repentance, and confession of any sin, any thought, action, or response that displeases God. Too frequently we overlook or choose to ignore those instructions forbidding covetousness, lying, and taking God's name in vain, and we give in to self and the lusts of the flesh. Repeatedly, we disregard His teachings about telling others of Jesus, fellowshipping with other Christians, bringing a tithe into the storehouse, and spending time with Him daily. We must ask God to examine our hearts and reveal any sin needing to be confessed. There may be habits or thoughts we've been accustomed to believing are allowable, yet they are offensive to God. Unconfessed, they cause us to become disobedient and shut us out from knowing God's will in other areas of our lives.

Secondly, it takes time, dedication, and perseverance. Noah didn't waver in his obedience even though it took 120 years to complete the ark's construction. We must diligently spend time reading and meditating on His Word to discover

His commands. A lack of obedience indicates a lack of faith. How it must break His heart when we only memorize and claim His promises! We treat Him as a jolly Santa Claus passing out gifts for our pleasure.

Perhaps the word *command* bothers you.

You don't like to be told to do anything.

The hair on the back of your neck starts to bristle when someone issues orders.

In fact, you were tempted to skip this chapter.

I could go back and insert the words *point, train, conduct, govern, guide, manage, regulate, rule, bid, direct,* and *instruct* to make this passage easier for you. But the message remains the same.

Our Lord commanded us to forgive as He forgives, to love our enemies, to do good to them who hate us, and to live lives of self-sacrifice. (*Self* is the root of all lack of love and disobedience.) Jesus called us to humble ourselves and become the servant of all.

Too often we connect obedience with full perfection. It hinders the Christian from thinking obedience is possible. We begin to question whether or not we really can be obedient each hour of every day, and we struggle in our

Christian walk. We mistakenly believe living a transformed life is impossible, and many stop short of breaking free of their cocoons and flying. None of us will be perfect until we see Him in heaven; but while passing through this life on earth, we can be obedient with the Lord's help. We must remember that while the Law demanded an impossible obedience, grace makes living an obedient life possible! When we obey the Lord in simple faith and love, our obedience is acceptable and pleasing to Him.

Scripture wasn't given to increase our knowledge.

God intended it to guide our heart attitudes, behavior, and lifestyles.

The Bible was designed to reach deep into our hearts and influence us to be holy, humble, loving, patient, and ready to do whatever God calls us to. The voice that commands us is the voice that inspires.

He will not require us to do anything that He will not enable us to do (Isaiah 40:29; 41:10; Philippians 4:13)!

When we discover a command and apply it to our lives, we gradually begin to practice new and more difficult instructions. Being conscious of our ignorance will make us teachable. Each time we're obedient—whether in large or small things—enables our faith in Him to grow and aids our metamorphosis. Slowly, step-by-step, as God observes our obedience, He reveals more of His love, strength, wisdom, guidance, and peace to us. And it's only possible with a loving, yielded heart.

The question is, "Do you *trust* Him enough to obey Him?"

When you don't know which job to take, what decision to make, and how you'll pay the monthly bills, will you choose to trust Him and obediently persevere in whatever He's instructed you to do? When the storms of life buffet you, when you feel as if you're going under for the third time, will you be determined to obey His commands...even when the going gets tough?

Obedience is a priority in Scripture—in the mind of God—and should be a priority in the hearts of His servants. We should examine our schedules and agendas to determine the priority we give our obedience to God. Have we given it the place of authority over us that God means it to have?

If we listen carefully for His voice and yield ourselves to the searching of God's Spirit, we may find we never gave obedience the proper attention it should have in our lives. Frequently, we are content to swagger along casually, unchanged, not realizing this failure causes the lack of power in our lives. Other times we knowingly indulge in pleasures that are contrary to the Lord's will. And we miss the blessings of God's grace and the full enjoyment of His love and nearness. They are beyond our reach simply because we never gave obedience the place of prominence in our lives God intended it to have. An obedience that pleases God is not necessarily seen in what we do, or don't do. It is manifested in the spirit in which we obey.

How do you respond when you discover one of His commands or when the Lord instructs you to do something? Do you deliberate, wondering what the results will be? We shouldn't be concerned with the results—God is responsible for the results. Our job is to be obedient. We shouldn't hesitate, question, or postpone responding to His instructions. Immediately obey. Every minute we delay in obeying God, makes it that much easier to disobey Him. Learn to obey at once! The struggle in delay steals the joy from the obedience.

There are no regrets in obedience. I would rather err, genuinely believing I was obeying His instruction, than miss His directions and become disobedient. Our ministry volunteers often tease me about my desire to be obedient even in little things, but I've learned the hard way. Only when I am completely obedient to Him will I experience peace.

You cannot disobey Christ and enjoy fellowship with Him at the same time. The more you value your relationship with Him, the deeper it hurts when you disobey Him.

Wholehearted obedience isn't the end, but the actual beginning of our learning process. We are simply to obey. We are to use all the strength we have and all the skill we can acquire in our obedience. We are not to depend on what we can see or feel for inspiration; we are to lean on Jesus and in the words He speaks into our hearts and in the Bible.

A heart yielded to God in unreserved obedience—nothing held back—is the one condition of growth in a changed life and in the spiritual knowledge of God's will. Any uncertainty about God's will makes joyful obedience difficult, if not impossible. Surrender, consecration, is of little value unless it means presenting yourself as a living sacrifice, *willing* to obey God's slightest command (John 15:10,14; Isaiah 1:19; Colossians 3:22-24). Perhaps we should take a lesson from Mary and spend time contemplating God's viewpoint of obedience.

Maybe a better question is, "Do you *love* Him enough to obey Him?"

4

CHERISHING MORNING PRAYER

And ye shall seek Me, and find Me,
when ye shall search for Me with all your heart.

Jeremiah 29:13

Mary yawned, stretched, and wiped the sleep from her eyes. Turning over, she noticed everyone was still asleep. She quietly slipped from her blanket, folded it neatly, and walked to the water's edge. She washed her face then sat back on her heels and admired the serene sea. The waves gently washed around her feet. She tilted her head and allowed the warmth of the sun to dry her face. Through half-opened eyes, she watched birds swooping down to catch fish. And they reminded her that she, too, was hungry.

Shaking the water from her feet, she turned and headed back to camp. Still no one stirred. Humming to herself, Mary began to prepare the food. From time to time, she'd glance up to see if anyone else were awake. Jesus was gone, but that wasn't unusual. It seemed to be His custom to go away by Himself early in the morning. Mary stopped her work and wondered where He went and what He did at this time of the day. She reasoned He must simply need some solitude.

As she continued to think of His time away from them, she remembered how tired He was each evening. Yet when He returned from these early morning meetings, He was both energized and peaceful at the same time.

Something happened at these appointments, and she wanted to discover what it was.

Should she follow Him one morning?

She decided it would be better to ask Peter or John where He went. Maybe they knew. If not, she was sure they would ask Him for her.

She worked undisturbed and soon had the bread, fish, and figs ready for everyone. Susanna was pleased to see the morning meal prepared when she awoke. She smiled at Joanna, acknowledging the beautiful job she had done guiding and teaching Mary. Laughing, she admitted her disbelief of the overnight change in Mary and praised her teachable spirit. By this time, the others were up, filling their cups with food. Good-naturedly they joined in, sharing their appreciation of Mary and teasingly wondering what they would have done without her.

Mary laughed with them, secretly grateful they noticed a difference in her, and went to sit next to Peter. As he made room for her, he noticed the questions in her eyes. "What now?" he wondered.

Even before he could say good morning, Mary bombarded him with questions about Jesus' early morning meetings. With a sigh, Peter began to explain where the Teacher went. He continued, between mouthfuls, to share with her some of the truths Jesus had taught them about the importance of early morning prayer.

Peter recalled the time when, after a day full of miracles and work at Capernaum (Mark 1:21-32), the crowd pressed in on them. Sick were healed and demons cast out. It was late before they got to sleep, but early the next morning, they found Jesus gone. In the silence of the night, He had slipped away to seek a place of solitude. They followed His footsteps, wet with the dew of night, until they found him *kneeling in prayer*.

Jesus chose to separate Himself from others each morning and commune with His Father.

Because He was subject to the law of humanity, He had need of continual refreshing and renewing. The Lord knew He was a Son, and the Father loved Him. He could not maintain the heavenly life here on earth without this precious time alone with God. His greatest need *and* greatest blessing of prayer was to spend time in silence and adoration communing with His Father.

Reaching for another fig, Peter glanced at Mary's face before he proceeded. As usual she was completely absorbed in everything he told her. Her rapt attention caused him to postpone responding to Andrew's call and continued to share with her. As the disciples listened to Christ pray and as they learned from His teachings on prayer, they discovered the main goal of His prayers was to glorify the Father. "…glorify Thy Son, that Thy Son also may glorify Thee" (John 17:1).

Peter paused and looked at Mary.

For the first time, she was speechless.

Her mind was reeling with thoughts about prayer.

Silently, she got up and walked along the shore, lost in hesitant, questioning, pleading prayer. Watching her seek understanding, Peter whispered a prayer for her.

> *❧ Can't you envision Mary's day*
> *beginning like this? ❧*

I imagine in Mary's quest for understanding the principles of prayer, she pondered the corporate prayers Christ's followers shared and the importance Jesus placed on His own time of solitude with His Father. I am confident that as she began to practice private communion with the Lord, she discovered His peace, His power, and His joy filling her and equipping her to live triumphantly in the midst of daily drudgery and struggles.

Prayer may be a mystery for many of us, too. While we desire to pray and sense the need to pray, we may not know where to start. Or perhaps in the past, it wasn't a vital part of our lives. It was ignored, neglected, or treated as a last resort measure. In our hesitation, we've become discouraged and placed prayer on the list of things we'll do someday.

Only someday never comes.

But when desperation, trials, and heartaches invade our lives, we immediately run to God in prayer. We want His help, guidance, and attention immediately. Unknowingly, we mimic the selfish child who cries, "Gimme, gimme, gimme!" How this must break God's heart.

Prayer was intended to be a fellowship time between God and His obedient servants. He desires it to be a conversation between two hearts, an interchange of thoughts. One listens and the other speaks and vise versa. Many have abused this special privilege by dominating the conversation with their own needs and desires. They refuse to be still and listen for God's guidance and instructions. Therefore, they leave their time of "prayer" empty, restless, worried, and confused.

There are others who hesitate to converse with God because they feel awkward, ignorant, or ill at ease. Our enemy, Satan, uses these emotions to trick believers and keep us from praying. He must block prayer for he knows the power we receive when we commune with God. Satan will use schedules, sick children, appointments, traffic, and many other interruptions to cause us to think we don't have time to pray. His victims also mistakenly believe that to pray they must use certain words, styles, or systems. But God isn't interested in our grammar, diction, or methods of conversing with Him.

He simply wants us to talk to Him!

It doesn't matter if we stumble over our words or offer eloquent praises, *the important issue is that we choose to pray!* He wants us to share with Him our deepest thoughts, hurts, desires, and details of our lives. He wants us to commune with Him about our successes and our sources of shame. Sometimes we may speak to Him as our Protector or Guide. Other times we may fall before Him in humble reverence calling Him Lord, acknowledging His rightful authority in our lives. Then there are the occasions when we cry out to our Abba, Father.

If we desire to live power-packed, changed lives, nothing can take the place of private and direct communion with God. I'm not saying we have to spend *hours* on our knees. God hasn't given us a minimum time frame. As I've researched the subject, I've learned that while all of the believers who experienced power in their lives and made an impact for God prayed, not all of them spent hours every day communing with the Lord. Some prayed with God simply, briefly, and expectantly each day. And God answered them! I believe we should be God-conscious at all times and continually be in an attitude of prayer about what is going on in our lives.

The indescribable bond formed during our morning prayer time joins us with God. We can be so firmly tied that, in spite of schedules, agendas, carpools, careers, and responsibilities, we remain focused on the Lord throughout the day. He becomes our sense of humor as we deal with little, muddy feet while driving carpool. He fills us with wisdom, equipping us to discern between distractions and priorities in our schedules. He is our strength as we juggle family, home, and job. His love fills us and spills over onto those we meet, bathing them in His presence. Weariness disappears. Discouragement vanishes. Confusion is replaced with peace. There is a spring in our steps, a twinkle in our eyes, laughter in our voices, and a joy in our hearts.

We are transformed!

If we view conversation with God simply as a duty or obligation, it will soon become a burden. If we see it as a means to secure our own happiness and safety, prayer will soon lose its sense of priority. Only a desire for fellowship with God will fill our hearts with joy and peace as we commune with Him.

Many in today's society want more of God—His love, His will, His holiness, and His power working in them, but they aren't interested in spending time alone with God. They want to live the transformed life, but they aren't willing to exert the effort it will entail. They casually use the term *spiritual* to describe themselves when, in fact, if they aren't spending time praying, they can't be filled with His Spirit. It's impossible to have His wisdom, love, peace, strength, and the knowledge of His will *unless* we have close personal communion with Him!

Even work in the service of God and of love is exhausting. We cannot minister to others without power going out from us, and this must be renewed each day. Just as the Israelites gathered the manna each morning for their daily food, we must also seek our nourishment and strength from above each day. Obediently, we listen for His instructions and willingly respond. We leave our quiet time alone with the Lord transformed, refreshed, and strengthened to face whatever comes our way.

Perhaps you genuinely desire to develop an intimate relationship with the Lord, but you feel inadequate, think you don't know how to begin, or believe you don't have the time it requires. Maybe you are a young mother struggling to find time to spend with the Lord or a businessman so overwhelmed with work even minutes alone are few and far between. You may honestly believe you don't have time to pray. And that's probably true. Most of us truly don't have time to pray. We *make* time! If you desire to live a Father-pleasing life, a transformed life full of His love and power, you'll choose daily to protect your time communing with God.

If we sincerely desire to spend time in prayer and take that first, tiny step of faith in obedience, He will bless our efforts.

He sees the intent of our hearts.

It's through prayer that we surrender ourselves to God each morning, acknowledging His right to our lives. When we think we're too busy to spend time with God and we rush headlong into the day without pausing to pray, we are actually announcing to the Lord that we don't need His guidance or help during the day. We mistakenly believe we can handle the day all by ourselves.

Satan whispers in our ears that we should put aside our Bibles and our prayer lives. He tells us our quiet times with God are not really important. All the while, he's scheming to take control, and when we fall for his tricks, we live independently from God. Another word for *independence* is *pride*. Another word for *pride* is *sin*. That's exactly the time we need to humble ourselves, repent and confess our sin, and yield our lives into His competent care.

Although we may hesitantly begin our habit of a morning time alone with God, soon we will cherish meeting with God, yielding ourselves to Him, and seeking to please Him. (Please see my books, *Redeeming the Time – Where Do I Begin?*, Chapters 3 and 4; and *Listening for His Voice*, for more prayer suggestions.)

Changed lives are possible. Breaking free from habits and practices that keep us bound to selfishness and pride is possible. Living a power-filled daily life is possible. Even though we might be required to sacrifice a few minutes of sleep, reschedule appointments, and prioritize this time above fellowship with friends, we must set aside time to be alone with God each morning. Those who desire to be like Him must begin by following Him in prayer.

As Mary watched Jesus, she recognized a change in Him when He returned from His time of solitude with His Father. She realized how important it was to Him. I wonder if it's important to you? If Christ needed it, how much more do you and I need it!

Mary discovered Christ-like praying in secret was the secret of Christ-like living in public.

Oh, may we learn that same lesson and be determined to apply it to our lives.

I pray we will hunger for a deeper relationship with Him. As we close our eyes in sleep each night, may we whisper a prayer asking God to awaken us each morning eager to spend time alone with Him.

We must realize the importance God places on prayer. We need our solitude with Him to confess our sins, get cleaned up spiritually, and listen for His voice. He desires to reveal more of Himself to us, to fill us with His love, to communicate His will to us, to change us, and

...to *wipe away our tears.*

5

ENDURING TRIALS AND TESTINGS

*Though I walk in the midst of trouble, Thou wilt revive me:
Thou shalt stretch forth Thine hand against the wrath of mine
enemies, and Thy right hand shall save me.*

Psalm 138:7

Mary's heart broke as she noticed the sadness in Jesus' eyes.

Although she hadn't been present, she had heard of the unbelief in Nazareth. Because of His love and concern for His friends and neighbors, He had gone home to Nazareth to share God's Word with them.

And they mocked and rejected Him.

Peter told her how the mob led the Teacher to the top of a hill and tried to throw Him over the side. Miraculously, the Lord was able to escape. As Mary recalled the hurt He endured when they angrily banished Him from His own village, tears formed in her eyes.

Now Jesus suffers more rejection and humiliation.

Mary couldn't believe her ears. How dare they talk to the Teacher in such a manner? Who did they think they were anyway? Pharisees and Sadducees? Peter whispered in her ear, "That's exactly who they are." Mary gave him a look of indignation and exclaimed, "Well, that's no excuse for trying to provoke Jesus. Didn't they know He only spoke the Truth?" Peter shook his head, put his fingers to his lips, and told Mary to be quiet and listen. Jesus skillfully answered their questions, which only exasperated them more, and they angrily marched away.

Mary wasn't naive. She recognized that everyone would not accept or love the Teacher as she did. She understood the Pharisees and Sadducees acted out of jealousy and fear. She knew the moneychangers and many evil businessmen resented Jesus and His teaching because it cut into their profits. All of them feared His power and authority to perform miracles. Secretly, they confessed a desire to know more about Him, but none believed in Him.

Her heart ached for them in their blindness.

As everyone sat around the campfire that evening, the meal finished, Jesus began to teach about testing and trials. Some of the apostles became distressed when Jesus quietly told them, "... in the world ye shall have tribulation: but be of good cheer; I have overcome the world" (John 16:33). The word Jesus used for *tribulation* meant *to crush*, *to press*, *to compress*, *to squeeze*. It carried the thought of grievous affliction and distress.

Time seemed to stand still.

The women stopped cleaning up after the meal and looked at each other.

Mary set the water pitcher aside and moved closer to Jesus.

The men listened intently.

They didn't like what they heard and wondered if they might have misunderstood the Teacher's meaning. Focusing only on the word *tribulation*, the men were shocked and dismayed. Bristling at the thought of enduring harassment, grief, and painful trials, His followers grumbled to themselves. They expected Jesus to set up an earthly kingdom, and they wanted to help Him oversee this kingdom. They didn't want to continue to face hardships, challenges, and danger.

They desired to follow Him, but they wanted it to be convenient and *easy*.

Knowing the thoughts of His weary followers, and knowing trials and testings would surely come into their lives if they were to continue the transforming process, Jesus wanted them to be prepared not only to *survive* the tribulations, but to *thrive* in the midst of them. He reminded them of His earlier teaching, "Come unto me, all ye that labor and are heavy laden, and I will give you rest. Take My yoke upon you, and learn of Me; for I am meek and lowly in heart: and ye shall find rest unto your souls. For My yoke is easy, and My burden is light" (Matthew 11:28-30). He was offering them rest for the soul—a freedom from fear, the supply of every need, and the fulfillment of every desire no matter what their circumstances.

So self-centered were some in the small group, they missed His promise to give them rest in the midst of the storms of life.

On this quiet night, He alone knew the trials He would soon be facing, the rejection, the beatings, the mocking, and the ultimate humiliation. He understood the cross was before Him, yet He never turned away from it. No one ever had more to disturb him, but never was He less disturbed.

He remained steadfast, fulfilling the will of the Father.

It wasn't easy for Jesus to endure the pain, the ridicule, the nakedness, and the sin of mankind.

It hurt every time the soldiers hit Him.

It jarred His body every time the cord struck His back.

The crown of thorns pressing on His head caused blood to drip down and mingle with the spittle from those mocking Him.

His body was raw and bleeding.

His face bruised beyond recognition.

Then they stripped Him naked and hammered nails into His feet and hands.

The Roman soldiers dropped the cross in the ground and lifted Him high, exposed to all mankind.

The sin of the world made Him feel alone and cut off from God.

His tribulation wasn't convenient or easy.

> ∾ *Maybe there was a teaching time around the campfire that night.* ∾

I imagine Jesus' heart experienced a range of emotions that evening. He knew how hard it would be for His followers to remain faithful in the midst of pain and suffering. I believe every thought He had and every encouragement He gave them was punctuated with the image of the cross. It loomed before Him. It must have been heavy on His mind. No one will ever experience the pain He endured. No one will ever suffer as He did. Yet He was ever thinking of mankind. As He taught His followers, as He shared with the woman by the well, as He gathered the children in His arms, as He ministered to the crowds, and as He hung on that old rugged cross, He didn't just see the Roman soldiers gambling for His garments.

He looked out and saw a world in need.

He saw you and me!

Just as Jesus faced trials and tribulation in His life, we also face difficulties, heartaches, and pain. And just as those sitting around the campfire recoiled at the thought of suffering, we too, respond in like manner.

Trials frighten us.

Tests intimidate us.

Tragedies horrify us.

We abhor the idea of suffering.

At the same time, we seem to be mesmerized by it. Volumes have been written about it. Bookstores are full of books on the subject. The media plasters it on front pages and pours it into our living rooms through the television and radio. Many times we go to sleep with pain as a companion and awaken to walk with agony throughout the day.

We cry out for relief. We seek advice from friends and medication from doctors, but find no release. Often we, like Peter, become so overwhelmed by the waves lapping at our ankles that our focus is drawn away from Christ; and we too, begin to sink. We long to be free from the misery but fail to reach out to the only One who can help.

Christ promises us rest and peace in our sorrows, but God doesn't remove us from our trials. He stands ready to preserve us *in the midst* of them. Many mistakenly believe the Christian life means deliverance from trouble. Their bubble is shattered when they discover it means deliverance *in* trouble, which is very different. All we have to do is reach out to Him. His yoke (joined with Him in an act of servitude) is easy and the burden, trial, or testing becomes easier to bear because the Lord is our yokefellow.

It's not the yoke, but resistance to the yoke, that makes the difficulty. Taking up His yoke means surrender of our will and heart to Him. And we balk at that principle. Often we'd rather struggle along on our own than yield to Him.

We refuse to trust Him in our heartaches and pain. And His precious rest is lost. But to the faithful ones who are willing to come under His authority and listen for His instructions regardless of the circumstances, He gives strength for every duty, courage for every struggle, a blessing in every cross, and the joy of life eternal in death itself.

> He walks beside us,
>   loving us,
>   protecting us,
>   even carrying us when necessary.

Tribulation, trials, and testing will come into our lives in all sizes and shapes and they will challenge our faith. Many today have lost their lives because they refused to renounce their faith in Christ. Others have been cruelly persecuted

when it became known they were believers in Jesus Christ.
Suffering surrounds us.

But for you, a trial could be an overflowing toilet, a flat
tire, a critical illness, an accident, or not being able to
conceive. For others, it could be the loss of a job, loss of a
loved one, or loss of health. Facing traffic each day, dealing
with an irate employer, and coming home to repair a
broken washing machine may be the test you face today.
Tomorrow, it will be something completely opposite.

No one is immune to tests.

Neither can we predict when and how they will come.

If we knew when the test was scheduled, we could prepare
for it. But it will always be different, and usually catches us
unaware. Trials are the tools God uses to test our faith in
His ability. Faith that isn't tested can't be trusted. That
explains where you are right this minute.

Do you trust Him?

Do you *really* trust Him?

If so, does your lifestyle prove that you do?

How are you handling suffering, testing, and trials when
they come into your life? Are you surviving under the
circumstances? Difficulties have a way of pushing us

beyond ourselves and into His waiting arms. Trials cause us to pray like nothing else can. It's there in God's presence that we find refuge from the heartaches of life. His arms encircle us, protect us, and hold us close.

Oh, precious believer, we don't have to simply survive *under* the circumstances. We have a choice. When we stay focused on the Lord, God enables us to live *above* our circumstances. And our actions and responses will prove Who is in control of our lives. His presence cheers the heaviest heart. Happiness may be a choice, but joy is a decision of the heart. Suffering shouldn't be looked on as a mystery, but a ministry—an opportunity to show evidence of God's abiding love in our lives.

How I cringe when I recall the tests I've endured so poorly...or failed. I learned the situation I was in could either make me kinder, more thoughtful, more dependent on Him, more gentle, more compassionate, strengthen my faith, *or* it could make me bitter, insisting on my way, focusing on the trivial, faultfinding, or full of regrets. It all depended on my relationship to God. The way we react to the trials in our lives reveals where we are in our spiritual growth process...and how far we have to go. When someone offends us, we can tell where we are spiritually by how long it takes us to forgive.

I'm so grateful that He takes my poor test results and gently, patiently uses them to rearrange my priorities, erases my guilt, and continues to transform me. The Lord doesn't ask us to be perfect. We will make mistakes. But our success is judged from His point of view, not the eyes of others.

When you face adversity, what is your response? Do you run from the problem with fear in your heart or do you stand and face it with the Shield of Faith (Ephesians 6:16)? God desires us to face each test in confidence and power knowing He is with us and He is in control. That's faith! And that's our shield.

God provides the wisdom we need for each challenge, the strength we need to do what seems impossible, and the protection we need from Satan's evil schemes. God is on our side!

In His wisdom, God uses trials, testing, and difficult circumstances for our good. Sometimes He allows a trial to come into our lives because of disobedience. He needs a way to get our attention, to show us our disobedience, and shape us up. Moses was forced to spend 40 years in the wilderness of Midian because he attempted to do things his own way. He wasn't satisfied to wait on the Lord's timing. God used this time of discipline to prepare him to lead the Israelites out of bondage. The Lord knew the difficulties Moses would later face and the training needed to accomplish what He had called him to do. Just as God used a negative situation in Moses' life, He can do the same for you.

Other times the Lord may apply pressure in the form of disappointments and pruning to develop our spiritual growth. We may already be living dependent, Christ-centered lives, but God recognizes that we need to move up another level. Using faith-stretching situations, He draws us even closer to Him. We are no longer babes in Him, satisfied only by milk; we are now ready for the meat of His Word, and He gladly meets that need. We no longer are satisfied to crawl. We step out on wobbling legs and soon learn to walk and to run.

There are also occasions when God permits suffering in our lives so it may be a testimony to those around us. As others witness our confidence in God, courage to continue on even though the way may not be clear, and commitment to Jesus Christ, they are inspired and challenged to develop an intimate relationship with the Lord.

I remember long hours spent in the hospital critical care unit waiting for information on my husband, willing him to survive his massive heart attack. Although my life seemed to come to a complete standstill, only revolving around those few minutes I was allowed to visit R.J., I was confident God was in control and He was working in my behalf to perfect, confirm, strengthen, and mold me into the image of His Son.

Surrounded by loved ones, I chose to use the waiting periods staying focused on the Savior and trying to point others to Him. What joy filled my heart as I watched my family and friends praying with other hurting families. We even started a "snack ministry," sharing the baskets of goodies we'd received with others in the waiting room.

This experience drew me closer to the Lord and mushroomed my trust in Him. Others continue to express the encouragement they received as they observed our family endure this difficult situation.

When we fail to learn a certain spiritual principle, we shouldn't be surprised if He allows another trial to arise. In God's school, He permits us to take the test over again and again…until we pass it! The Lord uses heartache and trials to grow us into the image of His Son. He knows trials bring out the impurities in our lives, much as heat brings out the polluted parts of the silver. The sullied, corrupt, tainted particles come to the surface and are removed.

God stands careful watch over us during the purifying process, as does a silversmith refining silver. He inspects the furnace constantly. For if the time necessary for refining is exceeded in the slightest degree, the silver will be injured. Our Lord is steadily intent on the work of purifying us; and in His wisdom and love, He only wants what is best for us.

He will not allow us to be tested beyond what we can endure (1 Corinthians 10:12-13). Periods of testing will come and go. Amid the heartaches and pain, we can take comfort in knowing the Lord will sustain us through the difficult times. He usually plans something we could neither see nor understand. He uses every test and trial in our lives to teach us something new about ourselves and something new about Him. Each trial has a unique way of drawing us closer to Him and revealing a more intimate understanding of God's attributes.

Nothing shows our hearts like a test. When we face the "trust" test, "security" test, "loving the unlovely" test, "discouragement" test, "dependence" test, "yieldedness" test, and so many more, the manner in which we respond reveals our spiritual maturity level. Trials and testing are purposeful in our lives. They prove the reality of our faith and build character. They strengthen us, discipline us, humble us, purify us, qualify us to help others, and prove to us the sufficiency of God's grace. Although some trials are very severe, believers are assured victory. Someday we'll see the reason. Our confidence is in understanding that God knows what's best for us now and is always working for our good.

The purpose of refining is to reflect His image.

Believe it or not, temptations are a form of testing. Some things in life are unavoidable—like death and taxes. Trials, testing, *and* temptations are also unavoidable. No one is able to elude them, especially temptation. Sooner or later it will come, usually sooner *and* later. Satan tries to pull our allegiance from serving Christ to aiding him. Quickly and skillfully, he undertakes his task with determination. Our enemy takes notice of times when we are tired, ill, or busy and cunningly uses these times to his advantage.

A temptation is a subtle form of testing. It is any enticement to think, say, or do something contrary to God's will. It may be a weak impulse or a powerful urge. A second piece of pecan pie beckons you. Skipping church to work in the yard is appealing to you. Certain magazines or television programs entice you. A neighbor sharing some juicy tidbit of gossip tempts you to join her remarks. You may be tempted to stay angry with someone, spend the day in self-pity, or be upset by a negative circumstance.

God allows temptations to come into our lives so we might demonstrate the supreme authority of Christ in our lives. The Lord doesn't allow Satan to tempt us for the purpose of causing us to fall, but that we might prove the superiority of Christ. The opportunity to do something wrong is presented to us. What we do with that opportunity is what makes it sin or not. With each temptation, we have a choice. Will we give in to the impulse of the moment or will we stand firm in Christ?

Every time we are tempted we have the opportunity to show the world who is in control of our lives. Is it Christ or Satan? We must remember, "Ye are of God, little children, and have overcome them: because greater is He that is in you, than he that is in the world" (1 John 4:4).

Only when temptation is resisted can we be strengthened. Before temptation comes into our lives, there may be innocence but never virtue. Innocence resisting temptation becomes virtue. The temptation is the fire in which the ore is refined into strong steel. It is choice that makes character. Character is developed through active resistance not just passive avoidance of temptation.

When we pray, "Lead us not into temptation," the prayer becomes the choice. It reveals the decision of our hearts. "Lead us" denotes we are following a Leader. We refuse to go alone. It also means we are yielded to His leadership in our lives. We are *willing* to follow. Jesus was tempted in the wilderness, and He withstood the Tempter and all his tricks. We are following behind the Victor over temptation!

The Lord urges us to, "Watch and pray, that ye enter not into temptation: the spirit indeed is willing, but the flesh is weak" (Matthew 26:41). Jesus urges us to be alert, watchful, and to pray. We are to prayerfully be alert to any action or thought which would cause us to act independently of our Leader. A temptation is a chance for victory if we never meet it alone, but instead you face it under the guidance of our Leader. It is during times of testing and temptation that we call upon God, and He shows Himself strong in and through us, and Christ's victory can be ours. When Satan knocks at the door of your heart, simply say, "Jesus, would you answer that for me?"

Being tempted doesn't mean you are a bad person or that your faith is weak. Rather temptation is to be expected in a Christian's life. That's why it's important for us to study God's Word and be familiar with His commands and promises. It's also valuable for us to understand because it is very easy to succumb to temptations and not even know that we are. We need to surround ourselves with godly influence of spiritually mature people—people who will be good role models.

There are two steps in victory over temptation. The first is recognition, recognizing that the situation presented to us is a temptation to do something wrong. Recognition exposes temptation. You identify that it's something to be resisted.

The second step is to plead the blood of Jesus Christ and stand firm. We can only gain victory over the tempter as we claim Christ's victory over him.

I often wonder how an unbeliever endures trials and heartaches. Where do they get their comfort? What keeps them going when everything in their lives seems to be disintegrating right before their eyes?

My heart continually aches for a Jewish friend of mine. She survived the Nazi death camp, Auschwitz, and all of its horrors. Liberated by the Allies, she made her way to Israel, only to be interred by the British. After a year in the British concentration camp, she was set free to become a soldier in the Israeli army. As unbelievable as it sounds, while on patrol one night, she was captured by the Arabs. She spent several months in an Arab prison before being ransomed by the Israeli government.

But the story doesn't stop there. Soon after her marriage, her husband was one of the first in Israel to be killed by a terrorist bomb. She has experienced a heart attack herself and buried her second husband as the result of a heart attack. She's had two retina surgeries, suffers from glaucoma, and now cares for her daughter as the young woman battles cancer.

My friend is full of sorrow, heartache, and pain. To her, there seems to be no hope. When told the disease in her eye might necessitate removing the eye, she wondered aloud how much more could she endure? She believes her life is worthless and yearns for some release.

I've shared Jesus with my friend. Several times. But she steadfastly refuses to listen and continues to painfully relive her trials. If she only understood His arms are waiting to cradle her. He desires to guard her nights with peace that comes from knowing and trusting in Him.

He longs to comfort her.
He wants to free her bondage to pain and regret.
He waits to *wipe away her tears.*

6

CHOOSING TO ABIDE

If ye keep My commandments, ye shall abide in My love; even as I have kept My Father's commandments and abide in His love. These things have I spoken unto you, that My joy might remain in you, and that your joy might be full.

John 15:10-11

Grape juice trickled down Mary's chin, but she chose to ignore it and popped another ripe berry into her mouth. Mmmm, they were delicious! Sitting in the shade of the vines, feasting on succulent fruit, and listening to the Teacher—she wondered if life could get any better than this. Content, Mary thought of the past months witnessing Jesus calm the storm, free the demoniac in the Gadarenes, heal the blind, ill, and lame. She recalled seeing the miracle of Lazarus raised from the dead and the sorrow of Jesus when He wept over Jerusalem. She marveled at the sight of power and compassion fused together.

Today the classroom was a vineyard. With a tone of urgency in His voice, Jesus began to illustrate a deeper meaning of the transformed life, the Father-pleasing life. Up until this time, He had mainly used the phrases, "Come unto Me" and "Follow Me." Now He gave them a new phrase, "Abide in Me."

Directing their attention to the vine, branches, and fruit, Jesus pointed out that, without the vine, the branch could do nothing. Patiently He explained that, without Him, they could do nothing. Believers can only be pleasing to God when they rely on the power of Christ dwelling within them. Jesus continued teaching and stressed that all the branch possessed belonged to the vine. The branch didn't exist for itself, but to bear fruit and make known the excellence of the vine. The branch has no purpose for existence except to be of service to the vine. He used this word picture to impress on them the calling of the believer and the importance of his consecration to the service of his Lord.

With this parable, Jesus taught the object of the union of the vine and branches. The branches were for fruit *and fruit alone*. Other trees may be planted for shade, wood, or to beautify the landscape. The vine is planted only for the fruit. And of each vine the owner expects more fruit.

Believers are to produce fruit!

They are to share God's love with mankind, pointing them to Jesus.

He went on to warn against simply trusting God for pardon and help, giving Him casual obedience, and neglecting to develop an intimate relationship with the Father. Over and over, He invited them to "Abide in Me."

Mary's heart pounded as she considered this new concept. Jesus seemed to be saying to her, "Thou are weak, but I am strong; thou are poor, but I am rich. Believe My promises. Yield yourself wholly to My truths and authority; just *trust* Me. I am the Vine, you are the branch. Abide in Me."

Slowly Mary rose and went in search of water to cleanse her stained fingers and face. As the water rinsed away the grape dye, she wondered what *abiding* fully encompassed? Jesus had explained *abiding* as allowing nothing in your life to separate you from God. *Abiding* also carried with it the confidence in God's unfailing presence and response to our requests or needs. Jesus was more conscious of the Father's presence than of the crowd pressing in to get near Him. When Christ was speaking to the crowd, He knew the Father was also listening. As the Lord healed the blind and lame, He felt the Father watching. Jesus was always conscious of God's presence.

Abiding meant choosing to live a dependent life. It meant recognizing that everything we are, everything we have, and everything we do is best only when it has God's direct touch on it. Mary remembered how difficult it was in the past to keep the most sacred vows.

Visions of past failures flooded her mind.

Hopelessness and tears of disappointment threatened to overwhelm her.

But then she heard His voice in the vineyard...and she turned toward the group. She could see His face lovingly encouraging His listeners to trust Him.

Suddenly, she realized the key to *abiding* was placing her *trust* in the Lord, not her own efforts! With renewed joy and freedom, she enthusiastically returned to the others. Her eyes now glistened with tears of joy.

With His help, she could learn to abide!

ê *I suppose it could have happened that way.* ê

I don't know about you, but for years I struggled with the principle of abiding in Jesus. I yearned to be one of those "mature" Christians who breezed through life seemingly undisturbed, without even a hair out of place. But as hard as I tried, I never quite mastered it. The illness of one of my children, a car accident, and a friend's fight with cancer all caused me to lose what momentum I had gained. I longed for that place of perfect peace. No matter what happened, no matter how difficult the circumstances, no matter how great the pressure, adversities, or the problems of life, I wanted the "peace of God which passes all understanding" (Philippians 4:7).

God has taught me so much in my journey as I learned to abide. Although the ability to abide in Christ was issued to me when I trusted Jesus as my personal Savior and Lord, *developing* it was a step-by-step process. When I discovered He didn't expect me to automatically know how to abide, that it was a learned habit, my feelings of frustration began to dwindle. I felt like Mary did when she realized that, with God's help, she could *learn* to abide. My frustration was replaced with confident hope.

With each new problem or trial, I learned to focus on the fact that the greatest problem in my life had already been solved. It was solved at Calvary's cross when Jesus willingly died for my sins. Keeping that in mind made all other circumstances pale in significance. No matter what I was facing or how discouraged I might become, as long as I was alive, God had a purpose for my life.

Imagine my subdued spirit when I learned simply *surviving* a period of testing and *abiding in Christ* were two different things. *Abiding* means *to remain steadfast and faithful, accepting the circumstances, and responding in a manner that glorifies God.*

If I wanted to abide, I had to learn to look at everything from God's viewpoint. I could no longer be cross and cranky when I discovered a flat tire, the toilet overflowed, had a car wreck, or suffered a headache. Abiding meant I needed to stay focused on God and His attributes in the midst of it all.

No excuses!

If I did so, my actions and responses would please God.

It wasn't easy, but I was learning.

Slowly, a moment-by-moment God-consciousness evolved.

Over and over again, as I endured my faith-stretching situations, God proved His faithfulness. Watching our small daughter struggle with pain as she recovered from surgery left me feeling vulnerable, helpless, and wondering "why" this had to happen to such a beautiful child. I stayed by her bedside 24 hours a day and, when the pain would become unbearable, she would cry, "Pray, Mommy, pray!"

Through my tears, I'd cry out to God to remove her pain and heal her body.

I readily admitted it was a miracle the doctors discovered her four separate, individual functioning kidneys, which the doctors chose to leave alone. But Elizabeth also had four malformed tubes leading from her kidneys to her bladder that needed to be replaced. The surgery was new and grave.

Doubt entered my mind.

How could I release this precious black-haired, five-year-old little girl and trustingly lay her in Christ's arms?

He seemed to say to me, "Just trust me."

And I had a decision to make.

Tentatively, I chose to trust.

It took faith—a faith in Someone bigger than me. That same Someone who had created the universe, held the stars in place, performed the miracle of the virgin birth, and raised Jesus from the dead.

I took a step of faith ... and He met me.

He didn't let me down!

The Lord protected our daughter during the surgery, guided the doctors' hands, maintained a careful vigilance during her recovery, and continues to lead her today.

I don't know what kind of week you've had, but if it has been a normal week, you've probably endured heartaches, problems, difficulties, and trials. Perhaps you've been depressed, disturbed, upset, or sitting on the "panic button."

What is your problem right now?

No money?

No friends?

No happiness?

No husband?

No wife?

No home?

There is a "no" something in everyone's life, and the "no something" has a purpose. God has a reason for it, and He asks you through the "no something" you think you lack, "Will you trust Me?"

Trust. A small, five-letter word becoming obsolete in meaning and usage in today's society. In most cases, people of integrity, honorable intentions, and responsible service are things of the past. Confidence in others, their abilities, and their intentions is at an all-time low. As a nation, we feel we cannot rely on others.

Although we seldom use the word *trust*, unconsciously we act on the principle of trust every day. We trust the chair we sit on will hold us. When we turn the key in the ignition, we trust the car will start. We trust the microwave will heat the water for tea, and we trust our paychecks won't bounce. On the other hand, we rarely trust the mail to be delivered on time or the auto mechanic to be completely honest with us.

An unbeliever gets his happiness from dependence upon some person, thing, event, position in life, or some measure of success. But for those who believe in Jesus Christ, God has provided perfect happiness in whatever situation we find ourselves because we *trust* Him. We do not need to know all the answers. In fact, there is no such thing as trusting God without unanswered questions. If we knew the answers, there would be no need to trust.

Trust is a place of complete dependence upon the One who is the source of joy and strength, the Lord Jesus Christ. When we don't see tomorrow's provision, when we don't understand why, when He asks us to wait, because we trust Him, we can face each new situation with confidence, trusting that the Lord is in control. Thoughts of hospitals and critical illnesses no longer hold us in fear. Lost jobs, deaths of loved ones, and moving to new locations no longer cripple us with depression or despair. God is in control, and we trust Him!

If our perception of trust is unfavorable, it's understandable that we're also confused about abiding. If we don't understand trust, we'll never grow to abide in Christ, and we will live shallow, empty lives.

Many today join with Mary and reluctantly admit their misunderstanding of the principle of abiding   They believe Jesus is their Savior and try to obey Him to some extent, but they've never realized their relationship with the Lord should be an intimate one.

Perhaps they do not know Jesus commanded us to abide in Him.

In their ignorance, they miss the blessings rewarded to those who choose to develop lifestyles of abiding. They observe other Christians serenely enduring everyday drudgery and responsibilities and heartbreaking trials, wondering why their own lives aren't filled with the peace that passes all understanding. Confused and discouraged, they muddle along secretly nursing a growing anger toward God.

Why does God allow suffering and trials?

Why does He permit us to run around bumping our heads against walls?

Why does He tolerate us hitting the "panic button"?

He allows us to go through all of these things so we will realize there is no peace in our lives if we are not abiding in Him.

Abiding is a foreign concept to today's lifestyles. We live in such a "hurry up" world. Computers, emails, cell phones, faxes, and pagers keep our minds swirling with information…and distracted from focusing on a moment-by-moment fellowship with the Lord. That's what abiding is all about—simply being aware of Jesus at all times and responding in a manner that pleases Him.

Many times, as we look back over the past week, we can see so much that could break our hearts. Then we stop and think of just how wonderful the Lord really is, how gracious He is. From all the pressures, difficulties, heartaches, and trials, there are only two reactions as far as those desiring transformed lives are concerned. We can choose to believe His promises, or we can choose to be miserable. We can either believe His Word and *abide* or we can hit the "panic button" and be miserable.

It sounds easy to talk about "abiding in the Lord" until we face problems and challenges – until we live, as so many are doing, in anguish and pain. Is it possible to abide then? Is it feasible to believe we can develop a God-consciousness and growing trust in Him regardless of our circumstances? Can we abide in the midst of troubles as well as in days of peace and tranquility?

I've learned that abiding in the Lord doesn't depend on external circumstances at all, but on my relationship to God Himself.

The growing pains were not easy, yet I know they were filtered through His hands of love. In spite of it all, I was bathed in His peace when my husband suffered a massive heart attack, our daughter survived a critical illness, a fire threatened to destroy our home, my mother experienced a stroke, our home's foundation became unstable and necessitated living in a hotel for three months, our car burned, my abdominal tumors had to be removed, my tailbone was broken, and chiggers had a feast on my legs!

Perhaps it's not in the difficult times that you struggle to stay focused on Jesus. Maybe it's in the daily responsibilities and drudgery. Diapers to change. Floors to mop. Laundry to put away. Meals to prepare. Routine, monotonous, continuous work. And we forget about the birds singing, the sun shining, the flowers blooming. We become so absorbed in our own routines, we fail to acknowledge God's presence.

If we aren't careful, the green-eyed monster of jealousy sneaks into our lives unaware. Susie has a new car. Mary just moved into a new, gorgeous home. Loraine has a personal trainer. Julie's hair is always perfect and so are her children. And before we know it, a heavy veil of discontentment settles in and steals our joy in the Lord. Any thought of abiding in Jesus disappears down the drain with yesterday's dishwater. We are miserable, and our enemy, Satan, is thrilled.

Evidence of abiding is seen as contentment. In the busy world we live in, being satisfied is quickly becoming a lost art. Although many of us may be resigned to our situations, we exhibit no peace or joy in them. We complain and whine. It takes too long for the hot water to fill the tub. The air conditioner isn't cooling well enough. Our car is too old. The yard is too small. Bedrooms too cramped. Clothes don't fit. It's too hot outside. It's too cold, etc. And to God's ears it sounds like a constant stream of whiners...much like the Israelites wandering in the wilderness.

It breaks God's heart for us to constantly complain and whine, for in essence, we are actually criticizing Him and His care of us. How dare we criticize the Creator of the universe? How do we have the nerve to complain about the One who gives us the very air we breathe? Thoughtlessly, irreverently, we murmur against the Lord when we should be praising Him for our countless blessings.

Contentment—joy in your circumstances—must be learned. It is an act of the will. It's an essential characteristic of the life of the believer who fully abides in Christ. It's graciously accepting the situation you are presently in. It's making a habit of saying, "Thank you ...," "I appreciate ...," "I'm grateful for ..." It's patiently trusting in your heavenly Father to work out a difficult circumstance. It's learning to join the apostle Paul and say, "...for I have learned, in whatsoever state I am, therewith to be content" (Philippians 4:11).

We expect God to perform miracles in crisis situations and often neglect Him in the daily responsibilities. But God wants to be glorified here and now, in the present minute, in each day of our lives.

✝⁄

Abiding is a gradual growth. It won't happen overnight. It takes time, and I've learned it takes more than reading the Bible and praying. It takes a day-by-day, moment-by-moment, *God-consciousness*. It is understanding that circumstances are never haphazard or accidental, but orchestrated by God to increase our knowledge of Jesus Christ.

> He's taught me to abide
>   one step at a time,
>   one precept at a time,
>   a little here,
>   a little there.

Learning to abide takes more than commitment, it takes surrender—giving up *all* to Jesus and trusting Him in *all* at *all* times.

The results are awesome!

Abiding fully in Christ is a life of exquisite and overflowing joy…regardless, in spite of, nevertheless!

A freedom comes into your life when you learn to abide. Your chains are broken. Bondage to selfishness, self-centeredness, attitudes of "what about me" are gone. You are no longer controlled by what the world thinks, but you live only to please God. You boldly step out in faith, regardless of the "imagined" consequences, and follow Him.

You're set free from your cocoon.

You're transformed.

You're changed!

Each day, as you experience His faithfulness, brings a blessing that makes surrender and trust easier to give. No longer are you bound with the cords of doubt, fear, and discouragement. The joy of knowing Him overcomes all the trials of life and

... wipes away all your tears.

7

REMAINING FAITHFUL

Fear none of those things which thou shalt suffer: behold, the devil shall cast some of you into prison, that ye may be tried; and ye shall have tribulation ten days: be thou faithful unto death, and I will give thee a crown of life.

Revelation 2:10

Mary tossed and turned restlessly. Unable to sleep, she pulled the blanket up around her chin. Looking up in the sky, she marveled at the brightness of the stars. They reminded her of candles flickering in the darkness. Gazing at the twinkling lights in the stillness of the night soothed her uneasy spirit and reminded her of God's faithfulness. He held the stars in place, caused the moon to shine at night, and covered them with the warmth from the sun each day.

Childhood stories of God's faithfulness began to flood her mind. Accounts of His provision of daily manna in the wilderness, water for the thirsty wanderers, and the miraculous dividing of the Red Sea helped her focus on the Lord God.

She remembered the times God delivered David from the brink of disaster. His victory killing a lion, wrestling a bear, and facing Goliath were familiar stories to all Jewish children. Fathers would dramatize the smallness of David versus the gigantic Goliath. Then they would emphasize that nothing was more important to David than his relationship with God. As he faced each frightening situation, David realized his faith was on trial. The lion, bear, and Goliath easily could have killed him. But David proclaimed his faith in God, and this was where he gained the victory.

Mary felt like she was facing a Goliath in her own life. Feelings of doubt and confusion gnawed at the corners of her mind. How could this be happening? Just last week the crowds in Jerusalem greeted Jesus with songs and palm branches. She had danced with the children in the streets. They hailed Him as King and followed Him as He rode through the city.

Tonight one of their own had betrayed Him. The soldiers surrounded Him, bound Him, and marched Him to the high priest Caiaphas's house. In shock and disbelief, she had followed them. The chief priests, elders, and the council held a mock court.

How dare they lie about Him?

Had their jealousy blinded them to the truth?

Her mind could not believe it when they sentenced Him to death. She turned to those around her and proclaimed, "There must be some mistake. The Teacher has done no wrong!"

But no one listened to her pleas.

Gingerly, she felt the bruises on her arms where the soldiers contemptuously held her back while they judged Him. She remembered how helpless she felt, as she watched them spit in His precious Face. And then they began to beat Him. Their tightly closed hands used Him as a punching bag, and each hit tore at her heart. She fought to free herself, but the soldiers laughed at her and held her tightly. She agonized over what was happening and thought He can't possibly endure any more. Then because it was close to sundown, they dropped Him into a pit reserved for prisoners condemned to die.

The soldiers released her, pushed her aside, and gave her instructions to leave. But she refused to move. Bravely, she stood there. The soldiers chose to ignore her.

What could she do?
No one would help her. Not even Peter.
She wept uncontrollably.
She spent the night
listening to the whip lashing Him,
fists pounding Him,
soldiers mocking Him.

It was quiet now. Perhaps the soldiers rested. Soon the sun would melt away the darkness. Surely, this horrible mistake would soon be corrected.

Mary sat in the corner of the courtyard waiting...

Suddenly, she saw them pulling Him forward. Caiaphas lead the way. Quickly, she dropped the blanket and ran to Jesus. Her stomach churned within her. So beaten was His face, she hardly recognized Him. She must comfort Him.

"I'm here, Teacher."

His eyes met hers and understood.

Courageously, she walked beside them to Pilate's hall.

She wasn't permitted to go further.

A crowd gathered. She searched for friends...anyone to help liberate Him.

Then Pilate appeared and offered to free Him, but the crowd refused and screamed, "Crucify Him!"

Slowly, Jesus came forward wearing a cruel, mocking crown of thorns and a purple robe. Pilate presented Him as King of the Jews. Mary held her breath.

The crowd and the chief priests insisted He be put to death.

There was nothing Mary could do.

Numb, she watched as they placed the cross on his shoulders. Struggling with its weight, He began the long walk down the Via Dolorosa. Even though the crowd pressed in on each side, Mary pushed her way along the street keeping step with her Lord.

Tears coursed down her cheeks.
Tears of horror.
Tears of pain.
Tears of disbelief.

Soon the soldiers were hammering the nails into His hands and feet. When they dropped the cross into the ground, His body lunged. Mary knew the pain was severe. She stood silently with His mother and Mary, the wife of Cleophas (John 19:25). Their presence was all they could offer Him now.

Then, triumphantly, He shouted, "It is finished!"

And He died.

Mary waited as Joseph of Arimathaea and Nicodemus took His body and quickly wound it in linen cloths and spices, as was the custom of the Jews. She followed them to the sepulcher where they laid Jesus, watched them roll a great stone to cover the opening of the tomb, and departed because of the Sabbath rest.

At dawn on the first day of the week, which was the end of the Sabbath, Mary and some of the other women hurried to the gravesite. They desired to continue the burial preparation begun by Nicodemus and Joseph.

When Mary arrived, she discovered the stone rolled away from the sepulcher. Quickly, she ran to tell Peter. She found him with John and told them what she had learned.

Immediately, they began to run to the tomb. And because John was younger, he beat Peter to the sepulcher. He stood there and gazed at the empty tomb. But not impulsive Peter. He didn't miss a step. He rushed past John and entered the sepulcher.

Indeed, it was empty.

Jesus was not there!

Digesting this new discovery, they slowly looked around and then went away.

But not Mary.

She stood beside the tomb, weeping.

The angels inside the tomb questioned her tears. She just wanted to find Jesus. As she turned aside, she saw the gardener. He also asked her why she was crying. She must find Jesus.

Then He called her name.

"Mary."

She recognized that voice. It's the same voice that called her so long ago. The voice that commanded the demons to leave her. The voice that forgave her sins. The voice that had been her Teacher these past three years.

It was Jesus!

The empty sepulcher which had filled her heart with grief, now made her shout for joy.

She fell at His feet and worshiped Him.

And tenderly, *He wiped away her tears!*

Then...He looked deep into her heart, saw that He could trust her (for she had proven herself faithful and trustworthy) and told her to go tell His followers He was alive and would soon be with His Father.

Quickly, obediently, she did exactly what He instructed.

He was alive and she wanted the world to know it!

❧ *Can't you imagine it happening this way?* ❧

How do you think you would have responded if you had been in Mary's shoes? Would you have been found faithful? Would you have remained at the foot of the cross? At the sepulcher when they buried Him? At the empty tomb?

Mary's deep love for her Deliverer held her at the foot of the cross and at the sepulcher. Is her example in vain? We will not fully live the transformed life until we understand the principle of faithfulness and join Mary in her desire to never lose sight of Jesus. She constantly sought His presence. And He rewarded her.

She was the first seeker on the morning of the resurrection, and she was the last. She came early while it was still dark, and she waited till all the others had gone.

Mary waited alone.

The other followers were with their companions in Jerusalem, mourning and weeping. Some of the women rejoiced at what the angels told them and left; but at the tomb, Mary wept alone…without a single friend.

✝

Loyalty isn't developed until we seek and find it for ourselves, and then testify to others what we've seen. If we sought Christ more in solitude, listening for His voice and responding, our testimonies would be more powerful. We wouldn't crumble, turn tail, and run when our faithfulness is tested.

It was in personally seeking Jesus that Mary received the glorious message to share with others. She sought and found Jesus for herself, and then Christ sent her as His faithful messenger to the others, the witness of the Lord whom she had seen.

Mary also waited fearlessly, for her love cast out fear in seeking Jesus. She overlooked the stigma attached to His followers as she waited in the courtyard and at the cross. She ignored the terrors of the night, going out of the city to the sepulcher for His burial. She disregarded the possible repercussions she might meet by returning to the tomb early Sunday morning. The others quickly came and left "for fear of the Jews." But Mary waited ...alone.

The angels in the tomb didn't frighten her. Their presence had filled the sepulcher with glory and awe to every other beholder, but Mary focused on finding Jesus. The stranger whom she took for the gardener didn't disturb her. There is no fear in love. She had but one thought. Where is Jesus?

The empty tomb no longer attracted her, Christ was not there. He was elsewhere. Loyally, she waited.

Fearless love,
   love that nothing could diminish,
      nothing could disturb,
         anchored her by the sepulcher.

Would you have waited?

Many people believe the journeyings of Jesus and His followers were full of excitement and interest. What could be more wonderful than to listen to the Sermon on the Mount. To witness the raising of the widow's son from the dead. To partake of the food miraculously multiplied. To be present when Christ showed mercy to the outcast and friendless and to hear Him overcome His adversaries by a wisdom they couldn't explain. But we need to remember that there must have been many days of hardship and discomfort. Sometimes Jesus was wearied and exhausted, sad in heart at the sight of misery, and distressed by the unbelief of the multitude and the hatred of the religious hypocrites.

It was not easy to follow Him day after day—to share His fatigues, grief, humiliations, and to become subject to the danger which loyalty to the Lord often involved. Following Jesus—when there wasn't time to rest or eat, when He spoke words that convicted His listeners and made them uncomfortable, when Christ's enemies took Him up the cliff to cast Him down, or when they tried to stone Him— was only possible for those who strongly loved the Savior and possessed a fervent faith in Him.

I wonder how many of us would have faithfully followed Jesus...in the difficult times?

Would the Lord find you loyal to Him today?

Has compromise,
a desire to fit into society,
an aversion to discomfort,
or an attitude of independence
caused you to be unfaithful to Him?

Perhaps, it's the fear of not being "good enough" that hinders your loyalty to Christ. When we are in the presence of holiness, there is a constant reminder of our insincerity, double-mindedness, self-righteousness, and conceit. All our sins are exposed. And we don't like it. It makes us uncomfortable. So we run from the Lord and become satisfied to remain bound with fear and disloyalty, missing the freedom available to us.

The secret of Mary's faithfulness was her ability to trust and obey God. She also realized that faith was progressive. What she learned in one situation, God later applied and reapplied to her life. To have the faithful devotion to Christ that Mary had, we must know Him as Savior, trust Him as Lord, seek an intimate relationship with Him, and constantly examine ourselves and our motives. Are they pleasing to Him?

We have the same Lord Jesus that Mary loved, and the same loving Redeemer. His love for us is not less than His love for her. It is equally true, equally intense, and equally constant.

Doesn't a love like His deserve our loyalty,
our fidelity,
our faithfulness?

Though none go with me, I still will follow.
Though none go with me, I still will follow.
Though none go with me, I still will follow.
No turning back.
No turning back.

8

BEARING A CROSS

I am crucified with Christ: nevertheless I live;
yet not I, but Christ liveth in me.

Galatians 2:20

Mary trudged along, determined to reach home before the sun set and darkness surrounded her. In the distance she could see the outline of Magdala. Thoughts of home, security, the love of her parents, her little sister, and a hot bath caused her to increase her pace. Closer and closer she came.

Finally she was there! The familiar sights, sounds, and smells surrounded her with memories. She was home! Her feet seemed to fly as she passed through the busy market. She quickly glanced at the merchants and waved. Excitedly, they tried to detain her, wishing to learn news from Jerusalem. But she deftly sidestepped them, explaining her need to see her parents first.

She hurried down the street toward her house and saw her sister playing with Simon's children. She called to her, and Abigail squealed with delight, stopped her game, and ran to meet Mary. Mary caught her in a warm embrace, held her close, and twirled around and around. Abigail laughed with pleasure.

Hearing the commotion, her mother came outside to investigate. What joy filled her heart when she saw her child. She called to Father to join them. Their daughter had come home. Picking up her skirts, she ran to meet Mary. Feelings of relief and gratitude coursed through her. They had heard of the crucifixion of the Teacher whom Mary followed and were concerned for her safety. But here she was, safe and sound.

Questions, answers, laughter, and expressions of love bounced back and forth as they affectionately greeted each other. With arms entwined, they entered their home to continue the conversation.

"How are you?"

"You look thinner."

"Are you hungry?"

"Have you come home to stay?"

"Did they really crucify Him?"

"There've been rumors that soldiers stole His body. Are they true?"

Mary barely had time to take a breath between questions. Her mother finished preparing the evening meal as they talked. Soon they were seated around the table, enjoying the food and being together again. Her parents glanced at each other and smiled. They remembered Mary as a laughing little girl, a tormented soul, a healed young woman, and now they had their precious daughter back. Satisfaction and contentment bathed their faces…and their hearts.

Much later that evening, Mary crawled into her bed. As she lay on the soft, familiar mattress, she remembered the past few years of sleeping on the hard ground with just a blanket to cover her. No bed. No pillow for her head. Just the companionship of loving friends, the light from a campfire, and the stars in the sky as a roof. She drifted off to sleep thinking about Joanna, Susanna, Peter…and Jesus.

Early the next morning she awoke to find two big, brown eyes peering at her. Abigail sat with her face in her hands, elbows on the bed, almost nose to nose with her. Mary laughed and playfully pushed her sister away. She quickly dressed and accompanied her to breakfast. Helping her mother in the kitchen felt good to Mary. She had left so quickly after Jesus freed her from demonic possession, she'd missed doing little things with her parents.

Spontaneously, she hugged her mother. She knew how often she'd broken her parents' hearts and caused them pain and sorrow.

But that was before she met Jesus.

Things would be different now.

The horror, pain, suffering, despondency, depression, anger, and discouragement were gone. Love, compassion, gentleness, thoughtfulness, and peace filled their voids and reigned in her heart. Mary was determined to demonstrate the difference Jesus could make in a person's life. With a twinkle in her eye, she picked up the pitcher and headed to the well for water.

Just getting to the well, filling the pitcher, and returning home became a daily feat. Remembering her healing, being fascinated by the transformation in her, and knowing she was a follower of the Teacher, caused everyone to stop and engage her in conversation. Patiently, she answered their questions, then hurried home to escape further interrogation.

Daily life in Magdala was not as easy as Mary had thought it would be. People didn't comprehend the complete change in her. For years they had seen her as a tormented, angry young girl. Now she was composed, confident, peaceful. They didn't understand. And what people don't understand, they don't like.

Many people mocked her for her faithfulness to Jesus. The Jews refused to believe He was the Messiah and accused her of blasphemy. The Gentiles enjoyed their lascivious lifestyle and chose to ignore the stories Mary told. Why, they reasoned, she was simply the demented demoniac.

Shrugging their shoulders, they excused any truth she might share.

Many days she longed to run away.

Run to Joanna for comfort and support.

Run to Peter and cry on his shoulder.

Run to Jesus and have Him *wipe away her tears.*

Meeting with the Lord each morning in prayer, she would pour out her feelings of defeat and frustration. "Why won't they listen to me," she questioned. Then she remembered ...they didn't listen to Him either.

Her knees calloused from time spent in prayer, and her heart broke from seeing their unbelief, Mary wondered how to share Christ's love with her mother, father, sister, and the others she met. How could she continue to respond in love when many of them were cruel and unkind to her?

As she wept tears of sadness on their behalf, it seemed that the Lord spoke to her heart. She remembered His words, "If any man would come after Me, let him deny himself and take up his cross daily and follow Me" (Luke 9:23).

"Lord, I'm trying to follow."

"But have you taken up your cross?"

"You mean I have to be crucified?" Thoughts of pain, suffering, nails, and blood flashed through Mary's mind.

"You have to daily die to self and allow Me to live through you."

"But, but … how do I do that?"

"Trust Me, Mary. I'll show you."

"Yes, Lord, I'm listening." And it seemed as if *He again wiped away her tears* as she responded to Him.

"First, you'll have to get rid of that proud, self-assertive, self-sufficient, self-confident, self-aggressive spirit and become completely dependent on Me."

"But, I don't have those characteristics …"

"Oh, yes, you do! And before I can guide you moment by moment, you'll have to do away with them."

"Yes, Lord," came her humble reply.

And thus continued Mary's internship in developing a Father-pleasing life.

❧ *Perhaps Mary did go home after the crucifixion.* ❧

Thinking of dying to self and being crucified causes confusion, fear, and trembling in our hearts just as it did to Mary. We genuinely want to make a difference in others' lives. We want to respond to people graciously and show them Christ's love, but dying to self? That means pain, and that's when we begin to back-pedal and back away from our commitment to unreservedly, fully follow the Lord.

The apostle Paul said, "I am crucified with Christ: nevertheless I live; yet not I, but Christ liveth in me" (Galatians 2:20). When we give ourselves to the crucified Savior, He comes to take up residence in our hearts. From that point forward, we have a choice to daily surrender ourselves to His control *or* to resist His authority in our lives. Although we may sometimes try to completely yield, our lives mainly consist of pleasing ourselves. Therefore, we become content to only know the cross in its power to atone. Part of us is forever whispering that it's expecting too much to always live a crucified life. After all, we're only human. Because we mistakenly believe we cannot *daily* live a Father-pleasing life, we become satisfied, while falling short of full surrender.

But if you want to know the power of a transformed life, you must understand there is a cross for the follower of Christ as well as for Christ Himself. A cross always means death. For Jesus, the cross meant a cruel death as a sacrifice for our sins. Our cross is the denying of self, death to self, for Christ's sake. It's the *attitude*, not the amount of suffering and shame we endure, that counts in God's sight.

Close your ears to Satan's lying whispers. Remember it is Jesus, the living, loving Savior, who Himself enables us to be like Him in all things. His sweet fellowship, His tender love, and His heavenly power make it a blessed joy to daily take up our crosses and follow Him.

Is there pain involved?

Yes.

But it's usually not the pain of the cross itself, but pain caused by the *reluctance* to daily practice taking up a cross and following Him.

Does it mean living as a hermit in the wilderness?

No.

It is manifested as we fellowship with others. True self-denial would be that no one would think of himself, but live for others. As we develop this lifestyle, it no longer becomes self-denial or self-sacrifice, it becomes a gift of love presented to the Savior because self-sacrifice is the very essence of true love. Forgetting self and your own happiness for that of another is a precious picture of Christ's love for mankind.

When we bear a cross, we willingly choose to leave our comfort zone. And that means we enter a *dis*comfort zone where all manner of negative feelings begin to bombard us. Feelings of inadequacy, rejection, and fear circle our minds as buzzards circle their prey. Thoughts such as, "I can't do this!" "What do I think I'm doing?" "What will I say?" "I don't want to do this!" render us trembling and ineffective. Often we decide to run back to our safe little boxes...

sitting there protecting ourselves, concentrating on ourselves, scared to death.

For the metamorphosis to continue, we must realize we will only grow spiritually if we enter the *dis*comfort zone! When we're out there, scared to death, understanding we don't know what we're doing, we yield to God and whisper, "I need You. I can't do this on my own. Change me any way You want. I surrender all." Then all the power in Heaven is released in us. And we discover—even though we didn't believe we could—we're doing things, saying things, witnessing to people, praising God, and pointing others to the Lord! "Not by might, nor by power, but by My Spirit, saith the Lord of hosts" (Zechariah 4:6).

Our daily responsibilities are the proving ground for this life of denying self, taking up a cross, and following the Savior. The relationship between husband and wife, parent and child, coworkers, neighbors, extended family, friends, and fellow church members are all opportunities for us to practice bearing a cross.

Jesus doesn't *command* us to take up a cross. He said, "*If* any man ..." and "...*let* him deny self." *If* and *let* indicate there is a choice to be made. There are obstacles to be considered before one *decides*. We have the privilege of choosing. We have the option. We are allowed to select.

We have a preference. Bearing a cross isn't a command, *it's a choice.*

Denying self and bearing a cross are *voluntary* options. When our loved ones struggle with cancer, leukemia, cerebral palsy, learning differences, broken limbs, or speech impediments, we can no longer use the expression, "That's just a cross I must bear." Not one of those conditions, or many more like them, are voluntary. None of us got on our knees and begged God to bless us with cancer or learning differences. Those conditions were placed in our lives *in*voluntarily. We didn't have a choice. I'm sure if given the option, none of us would choose to suffer these conditions.

What then is a cross? Remember, it's voluntary. Instead of going shopping with a friend, you choose (without complaining) to baby sit with a neighbor's children so she can visit a friend in the hospital. It's not easy. The children take constant supervision, snacks, diaper changes, and toys. But you do it.

Discovering a child in your Sunday School class can't attend church the next few weeks because his mother no longer has a car, you choose (without becoming a martyr) to leave home early and pick him up. It's not easy. You have three children of your own to dress and bring to church. But you do it anyway.

A friend of yours is dying of cancer. On your way to work each day, you choose (without drawing attention to your actions) to visit her in the hospital. Some days she's asleep when you arrive. You write a note on a napkin telling her you were there. Other days, she's awake and you cry together. It's not easy, but you rearrange your schedule to do it.

Another friend learns her estranged father is dying of cancer. She determines to reestablish a relationship with him and tell him about Jesus. To do so, once a week she must get up early, leave her husband to take their three girls to school, and drive three hours to her father's home.

Giving the caregiver the day off, she cooks, cleans, and loves an angry, old man. At the end of the day, she wearily crawls into her car and drives three long hours home to begin caring for her own family. And each Thursday when she finally turns into her driveway, you are standing there with dinner for her family. It's not easy. You have a husband and children of your own, and you're busy, too. But you want your friend to know that you love her, and you're there for her. So you do it.

Bearing a cross is choosing to set aside the magazine you want to read, and helping the worn out mother next to you entertain her sick child. It's taking food to a neighbor when they need encouragement, mowing a friend's lawn when he's ill, listening to a heartbroken acquaintance repeat herself again and again. It's calling a friend who has just lost a loved one when you don't have the funds for the long distance call. It's staying up late to wait for your husband after a hard day at work. It's getting up early and having the coffee ready when he leaves each morning.

It's giving up attending the church service and working in the nursery. It's choosing not to have your nails done any more and donating the money to a missionary. It's taking time to run an errand for your husband when you have a million things on your own agenda. It's missing the final episode of your favorite television program to read to your child.

It's dying to self.

The heart of sacrifice is that it's voluntary, and that it really costs you something. It's a choice—made joyfully, with no reservations. Bearing a cross means doing something, or doing without something, so help may come to another, even though it cost you some real personal suffering of spirit or body (or both) or lack of what you should have and would enjoy. It's doing something when you don't have to ...except the have to of love. It's a heart attitude.

You may think, "But I can't!"

Oh, yes, you can!

He'll teach you. He'll guide you. As you *choose* to take up your cross, He'll be your strength, your courage, your peace. He'll be right there beside you every step of the way.

> *The cross before me, the world behind me.*
> *The cross before me, the world behind me.*
> *The cross before me, the world behind me.*
> *No turning back.*
> *No turning back.*

9

SEEKING DISCERNMENT

If any of you lack wisdom, let him ask of God, that giveth to all men liberally, and upbraideth not; and it shall be given him.

James 1:5

The lamps from the houses didn't shed much light in the darkened streets, and Mary was grateful the little oil lamp she carried gave enough light to see one step at a time. Soon she would be home…and in bed.

As she walked, she thought back on the past few weeks—long, grueling, backbreaking, energy-draining, often confusing weeks. And she began to pray, "Lord, I don't know what I'm doing. I'm so tired I can't think straight. I need Your help. I arise before dawn to have my time alone with You and each day it's way past my normal bedtime before I crawl into bed. *Normal bedtime?* I've even forgotten when that was! Last night, I fell asleep at the table talking to my parents, and mother had to help me to bed.

Not only am I tired, but my mind won't work clearly. Am I doing too much? You know I didn't solicit all this work. People came to me. At first it was the young, single women, then it was the married women. Now it's mothers and sisters and children. They all want to know what caused the change in me. They desire to have the peace I have (right now I don't feel very peaceful, just tired).

They ask me about my prayer time with You, how to get along with those in authority, and how to deal with jealousy and resentment. One woman asked me how to be a godly wife. I didn't know how to respond. I wanted to say, 'How would I know? I'm not married.' Thank goodness I didn't. I heard myself sharing with her all Your teachings on love and forgiveness. She seemed to understand, but should I have replied differently? What would You have said? Fill me with insight because now she comes to visit *and* brings two friends with her! How will I ever be able to answer their questions?

Mothers have started bringing their children over in the afternoons. They want me to teach them (can you imagine *me*, a teacher?!) the importance of obedience, integrity, honoring their parents, and truthfulness. At first there were only four or five little ones. Now about twenty-five vie for a piece of my lap. I find myself hugging sticky faces, playing games, and sitting in the middle of a sea of inquisitive eyes. They want to know why the stars come out at night, why butterflies have soft wings, and why honey tastes so sweet. We laugh a lot, and I love each one of them. I'm trying to answer each question and teach them about You. Help me remember everything You taught us. I recall the way You called the little ones to You and held them in Your lap. Oh, I want to share Your love with them.

I know it's a wonderful opportunity—not just for the children but for their mothers, too. *The mothers don't leave.* They sit in the background, not visiting with each other, but listening to every word I say. Help me say the right things! Enable me to show them how much You love them. When the children leave, may they know how special they are to You, and may those mothers come to understand how valuable their precious children are to You.

Speak to my heart, Lord. Remind me of Your teachings. Fill me with insight and wisdom. Give me discernment! Don't let me be confused or drawn away from the truths You shared with us. Help me take advantage of every opportunity You present. Don't let me become so weary that I'm distracted from staying focused on You. Be my strength. I *need* You. In Jesus' name, Amen."

Mary opened the door to her parents' home and entered with a renewed energy and strength. She greeted her mother warmly and began to share the events of the day with her. Before long, her father and Abigail joined them. She watched their faces as they listened intently. She knew they were falling in love with Jesus!

Her parents wanted to hear all the details of the day. Where did she go? Who did she visit? *What did she say?* "Yes!" Mary thought—it was the exact question she was waiting for. She delighted in sharing with them the miracles of Peter walking on the water, the feeding of the five thousand, and the healing of the man with the withered hand. The expressions on Mary's face and the way she used her hands almost made the stories come to life. Her parents nodded in amazement and later talked among themselves as they prepared for bed.

Thus began a pattern. Each night when Mary returned home, she discovered her family eagerly waiting for her. And the teaching continued. After she described the events of the day, and saw that their interest was high, she began to share Jesus' parables: of the wheat and the tares, of the lost sheep, of the forgiving king and the unforgiving servant, and so many more. Their questions initiated lively discussions with Mary praying fervently for wisdom.

❧ *It could have happened that way.* ❧

Have you ever been in a situation similar to Mary's? Desperately desiring to share the love of Jesus with someone and sincerely not knowing how? I have. In the mall, I've watched frustrated parents discipline their children in a manner not pleasing to God. At church, I've seen adults so engrossed in themselves and their agenda that they ignore a hurting individual sitting right next to them. While traveling, I've observed lonely, confused people drowning their problems in mixed drinks. I've watched teenagers respond disrespectfully to their parents and other adults. And the list goes on and on.

What should I say?

Will they even listen to me?

How do I make a difference?

I've received letters from husbands whose hearts are breaking because their wives have left them and their families have been torn apart. I've had telephone conversations with women, pouring out their innermost feelings, who expect me to respond with "wisdom" and tell them how to solve their problems. I've listened to young mothers tell of their fear of rearing children in today's Godless, violent, immoral society. I've watched a depressed, discouraged mother sink to the floor, overcome by tears. Wives are concerned about the temptations their husbands face and the public's acceptance of extramarital affairs. Divorce is common. Most families today are fragmented. And they all want answers.

How should I respond?

Will they accept what I have to say?

How do I point them to Jesus?

I've sat in meetings with computer geniuses and financial wizards. They might as well be speaking Russian or some other foreign language to me. I've listened to real estate agents explain several options and then turn expecting me to immediately, intelligently reply. I have no idea how to respond. I don't even know what the conversation has been about!

I sat next to my little daughter's hospital bed and looked into her searching eyes while she waited for me to say something to take the pain away. I sat in hospital waiting rooms, surrounded by friends, as my husband battled for his life, and I struggled for the right words to keep us all focused on Jesus. I sat close to my mother in the nursing home and searched for words to comfort her confused mind.

Have you ever been there? Ever wondered what to say when the doctor announces you have cancer? Your teenage daughter confides she is pregnant? Your alcoholic brother is placed in jail? Your friend tells you she's on medication because of depression?

Ever wondered what to say to your child as he walks off the field having lost an important game? Ever contemplated how to respond when your teenager has his first car accident? Your husband loses his job? Your son fails his college entrance exam? Your pet dies? The house burns? Granddaddy passes away? You have a flat tire? The toilet overflows? All three of the kids are ill, and the pharmacist can't understand why you've misplaced your checkbook?

If you have days like I have, you've probably experienced all of the scenarios mentioned on the previous page. And like Mary, you join me in desiring that our answers and responses point others to God. We don't want to have to deal with regrets and wasted opportunities.

I long for discernment!

For clarity of thought.

For acuteness of judgment.

I desire more than just head knowledge.

I want wisdom. I want to know what is right and understand the correct response and action in every situation.

Knowledge is just an acquaintance with facts, truths, or principles. It may be gained from study or experience. Wisdom is knowledge that is rightly used. Knowledge may make excuses for a lack of understanding or foolish actions, but wisdom circumvents them.

Many people are very knowledgeable half an hour after a situation, but to be filled with wisdom is to be able, at once, to apply knowledge rightly in all circumstances. Wisdom enables us to bring our knowledge into practical use in our daily lives. It gives us a sense of the right thing to say to fellow believers as well as those who don't know Christ as Savior.

We need wisdom to conduct our affairs in a manner which will bring glory to God's name, for mere knowledge will not enable us to do so. Wisdom comes when knowledge is guided by the Holy Spirit. Then we may know what the will of the Lord is in our homes, recreation times, careers, and church. It will guide us as we speak to heartbroken friends, aid us as we present the Gospel, and give us clear thinking as we make decisions. Wisdom is the application of knowledge based on a moment-by-moment sensitivity to God's presence.

I know many people who are scholars. They are adept at physics, medicine, computers, science, literature, and Bible truths. Some know much, but understand nothing. They implicitly accept what they are taught without examining it or understanding what the heart of it is. Thus they become uninformed, unaware, and unlearned.

Spiritual ignorance is a constant source of error, inability, and sorrow. If we do not know the will of God, how can we do the will of God? If we are ignorant of the truths of God, we become the prey of any false teaching to which we are exposed. Ignorance will cause us to run risks, lose opportunities of usefulness, and fall into dangerous mistakes.

In the metamorphosis of a transformed life, we come to understand that we must know Jesus Christ as Savior before His teachings mean more to us than lofty ideals. We discover that Jesus Christ did not come to teach only. He came to make us what He teaches we should be. Through Him, by allowing Him full access to our lives and realizing our own inability, *He* can change us.

God desires to fill us with His wisdom and discernment. But all too often, we quench the work of the Holy Spirit in our lives, and we become desensitized to His voice. Unless we are living in fellowship with God, our sins confessed, we will not hear His directions. The Holy Spirit gently nudges, trying to steer us to the right course. His voice is so small, so soft, only those who are listening can hear.

Many miss hearing His voice because they rely on past experiences—the day they gave their heart to Christ or a moment ten years ago when the Lord guided them—and they live on memories, missing His guidance in the present. For the Holy Spirit to speak to our hearts, we must have a moment-by-moment relationship with the Lord.

Holiness of heart will increase the illumination of our minds.

Whenever the Spirit pricks our hearts, we must learn to stop immediately and examine the situation. What is God trying to say to us in our present circumstances? Is there sin to be confessed? Then confess it!

Often it's easier to hear God when we are on the mountaintop of spiritual victory. But when we are in the midst of trials and suffering, we must listen carefully for His voice. If we choose to ignore His gentle push and don't respond to it, we unconsciously continue to grieve Him…and we miss His guidance in our lives.

Our desire to live the transformed life—stepping solely within the will of God for our lives—begins with a desire to hear what He is saying. When we are confused about where God is leading us or are not clear about what He wants to change in our hearts, *listening* is the first and most crucial element to a changed life.

The will of God concerns the present more than the future. The Lord desires that our attitudes and actions be pleasing to Him. Therefore the little decisions we make every day— even more than the big ones concerning the future—are important to Him. We have very little control over the future. There are no guarantees about tomorrow. We need only to be concerned with knowing and doing His will in the *present moment*. Nothing else really matters. What does the Lord want from me right now? Call a friend? Write a note of encouragement to someone? Take food to an overwhelmed, young mother?

We must be obedient in the things that we know He wants us to do at the present time, or we will never be able to hear His voice directing us. We know He wants us to trust Christ as Savior. Fellowship with other believers. Tithe. Observe Communion. Set aside time each day for prayer. Meditate on His Word. Obey His commandments. Therefore, we must obey these commandments before the Lord will reveal any more of His will to us. We should not stop with simply understanding who Jesus is and what He's done for us. We should, like Mary Magdalene, yearn for more.

How do we gain wisdom and godly discernment?

By seeking to live a life which pleases the Lord,
   meditating on His Word,
     spending time in prayer,
       and listening for God's voice
         as we go about our daily responsibilities.

10

GUARDING THE HEART

Let the words of my mouth, and the mediation of my heart, be acceptable in thy sight, O Lord, my strength, and my redeemer.

Psalm 19:14

Sitting on the corner of her bed, Mary leaned her head against the window and watched the sun slowly peeking over the rooftops. She took a deep breath, exhaled, and marveled at the beauty of the sunrise. She loved this time of day. It was so quiet and peaceful. No one was stirring. Nothing to distract her thoughts from the wonder of God's power and creation.

Hearing a step in the hallway, she finished her prayer time, quickly dressed, and went to help her mother with the morning meal. As they worked, they chatted about the responsibilities of the day. It was Friday, and there were many preparations to be made for the Sabbath. Mary agreed to go to the market and purchase food while her mother and Abigail made the arrangements at home.

Picking up the water pot, Mary hurried to the well. It was early, so she walked alone. Engrossed in her thoughts, she fairly flew along the path. Mary wondered how she would get everything done. Nothing was eliminated from her schedule, just more added to it. She was trying to be an obedient daughter. She was trying to honor her parents; but if they asked her to do one more thing today, she thought she'd scream.

She quickly filled the pot and started for home. Carefully carrying the water so it wouldn't spill, Mary rehearsed ways to decline any more tasks today. She rounded the corner and almost collided with Hannah, Sarah, and Miriam as they headed for the well. They laughed and tried to detain her with conversation about Sarah's upcoming betrothal. They were in no hurry and enjoyed teasing Sarah about the cooking, housekeeping, and laundry she would soon have to do. Smiling, Mary continued toward home, explaining how busy she was today.

As they parted, Mary thought she overheard them whispering about her. Her mind raced. If they wanted to talk about her, just let them, she had better things to do. In fact, she had a million things to do.

But Sarah did look beautiful this morning. Mary thought about her long, dark hair that gleamed in the sunlight. And her big brown eyes that glistened when she spoke of Simeon. Sarah was tiny and petite. Gentle. Smart as a whip. Creative. And she was going to be married! Sarah was all the things Mary wasn't. Enviously, Mary trudged along dreaming of a time when she would marry and have a family.

She entered the house and plopped the water pot on the table, gathered the basket for the market, and pouted as she left again. The weight of the basket seemed unbearable, and it was empty! Her whole body ached and balked at the thought of the rigors of the day. Sometimes life just wasn't fair. She was trying her best, and her best never seemed good enough.

The day progressed slowly. Mary taught the children's class, but she was tired and impatient. The little ones seemed to get on her nerves today. Even though she tried to keep a smile on her face, their constant questions irritated her—sometimes the same question over and over. And their mothers were no help. They just sat there watching her deal with the children.

When the last one left and the yard was quiet, Mary sat in the shade of the tree to rest for a moment and ponder the events of the day. "Lord, what is wrong with me today? I love these children, and I love their questions because they give me the opportunity to share about You. They are usually a joy to be around. They weren't any different today than any other day. And their mothers never help me. It must be *me*. What is going on?"

"Do you really want to know?"

"Yes," Mary answered, genuinely puzzled.

"Your heart attitudes stink."

"My *what* does *what*?"

"Your heart attitudes are not pleasing to Me."

"What do You mean? What have I done to displease You?"

"Well, get a quill and parchment and I'll tell you. It is a long list."

Heartbroken, abashed, and ashamed, Mary hung her head and tearfully listened as the Lord brought the events of the day before her eyes. Jealousy, envy, and pride strutted through her mind waving red flags. She had fallen flat on her face. She had sinned. With remorse, she repented realizing that, although her sins didn't change her relationship with God—she was still His child, they broke her fellowship with Him. She confessed each one, agreeing with God that they were wrong, and asked for His forgiveness.

Mercifully, He forgave her,

   wrapped His arms of love around her,

      ...and *wiped away her tears.*

❧ *Perhaps Mary did have a bad day.* ❧

Ever been in Mary's shoes? Do you know *exactly* how she feels? One minute your sailing through life, including testing and trials; and the next minute, you've made a mess of things and find yourself sitting in the middle of the floor, crying. I have. Not just once, but on many occasions.

I'm sure Mary had days filled with regrets because of wrong heart attitudes. She was human just as we are. And as long as we live on planet earth, as long as we reside in these fleshly bodies, we will make mistakes and need to examine our hearts' positions and responses…daily.

Heart attitudes, responses from the heart, and the condition of your heart are all phrases used to describe that innermost part of an individual, the hidden man of the heart (I Peter 3:4a). It is the real person, inside the body, who has been born again through faith in the Lord Jesus Christ. It's the way we view things and situations. And if our hearts are right, our actions will be right.

We may be doing everything in our lives seemingly correct. We're obedient. We're on time to church. We tithe. We clean up after the children's choir performance. We go on mission trips. We even volunteer to be youth camp counselors. Yet sometimes, when God observes our lives, He's disappointed in us. His x-ray vision penetrates the outer shell of our bodies and zeros in on the heart of the matter. He examines *why* we did what we did.

He saw that we were obedient, but we resented it. He noticed our attendance in church, but He also recognized the way we criticized those around us. Helping clean up after the children's choir performance was useless in His eyes because we were busy judging others for not volunteering. Going on mission trips and serving as camp counselors were worthless actions from His viewpoint because we weren't really interested in helping others, we just wanted people to think more highly of us.

And the list goes on. Susie gets a new car, and we are secretly jealous of her. Marie is asked to teach a Bible study and, in the recesses of our minds, we wonder why? We believe we are so much better qualified. We wear ourselves out taking food to friends who've been ill simply because we want to impress them with our thoughtfulness. Publicly, our prayers are long and eloquent hoping to influence others with our spirituality. We are submissive wives, yet complain under our breath. We look at ourselves through rose-colored glasses and use a magnifying glass on everyone else.

We can do the right things with the wrong motives. When we examine our motives, we realize we have hypocritical, judgmental, proud, presumptuous, and deceived hearts.

And our attitudes stink!

Often we are so busy playing "church," involved in Bible studies, volunteering on committees, and teaching Sunday School classes that we don't even notice bad attitudes creeping into our hearts. Slowly they infiltrate, find nooks to settle in, and begin to control our actions. For a while the world may think we are "Miss Wonderful," "Mrs. Super Christian," or "Miss Pollyanna Always Happy," but behind our tired masks, lurk hearts filled with pain and confusion that cannot be hidden forever.

No one knows what goes on behind the closed doors of your life. But God knows. He sees if we are full of pride or humility. He recognizes if we have a "me-first," selfish attitude or a servant's heart. He observes the secret sins tucked away in our hearts. While our actions may be disguised, our motives cannot be camouflaged from His view.

Before long, our actions tell the world the condition of our hearts. If we say we are stressed, we're telling the world we have no peace in our lives. If we express our anger, we are giving evidence to those around us of our animosity. If we criticize others, we affirm a judgmental attitude. If we complain about our circumstances, we declare our ungratefulness. Peace and stress cannot lodge in the same heart at the same time. Anger, complaints, and criticism cannot be present—at the same time—in a heart filled with God's love. Jesus Christ didn't die on the Cross so we could live stressed, angry, judgmental, whiney lives. He came so we might have abundant life—full of joy, peace, strength, and wisdom.

My prayer before I speak is always, "Let the words of my mouth, and the *meditation of my heart*, be acceptable in thy sight, O Lord, my strength, and my redeemer," (Psalm 19:14, italics mine). That's the key to living the transformed life! Heart issues! From the heart pours forth the words of our mouths. If our hearts are yielded, sensitive to God's voice, full of His love, the world will know it. Our family will know it. Our friends will know it. They will not doubt Who is in charge of our lives. They will be able to recognize God's peace filling us and guiding us through difficult situations. They will hear His words of love and comfort and wisdom flowing from our mouths. And His name will be glorified.

Throughout Scripture, God stresses the importance of heart attitudes. Yet rarely do we heed His warnings. "Keep thy heart with all diligence; for out of it are the issues of life" (Proverbs 4:23). The Lord urges us to guard, protect, and preserve our hearts—our innermost thoughts. He wants us to garrison our hearts, keeping them tender and sensitive to His leading. And He knows it will be hard to do. That's why He instructs us to guard our hearts, not to make life difficult, but to protect us. Living in a world of violence and pain with little attention given to God, His love, and mercy, we tend to become calloused and hardened dealing with events in our daily lives.

With rigid, hardened hearts, we are poor testimonies of God's love. I think of my Jewish friend whose heart is hardened toward God, and then I also remember a friend whose heart—because of her choice—is tender toward God. When told of the murder of her teenage son, my friend shared with me that her constant prayer request was, "O Lord, don't let my heart become hard!" And He answered that prayer. Not only did she stand at the trial during the sentencing and, from a heart filled with God's love, forgive the murderer, but today she continues to be sensitive to the needs of others, loving, giving, and kind. She chose to guard her heart.

Over and over God exhorts us to inspect our hearts daily. In Psalms, He warns us that He will not tolerate a proud heart. In Deuteronomy, God admonishes those with presumptuous hearts. In Romans, He speaks of those with hypocritical hearts—those who judge others but not themselves. In Matthew, the Lord tells of the phony heart. In other places, He stresses the despising heart, complaining heart, critical heart, troubled heart, lustful heart, obedient heart, and on and on He goes. Deliberately, God repeats the importance He places on the conditions of the heart.

In several places He emphasizes the importance of not being faint-hearted. A person who is fainthearted lacks courage, is full of fear, and is easily frightened. Because the Lord knows our feeble flesh, He knows how easy it would be for us to give up when the going gets tough. God never promised there would be no adversity in our lives. No one knows that better than we do. As we go about our daily lives being moms, housewives, nurses, doctors, secretaries, salesmen, truck drivers, accountants, plumbers, or nursery workers, we face difficulties and pain. If we are faint-hearted, we lose our strength and courage and we grow weary, becoming stumbling blocks to other Christians. They look at our pitiful, fearful lives and see no reason to serve the God we say we love and worship.

How do we guard our hearts? By *choosing* not to deliberately expose them to anything not pleasing to God. It will mean choosing to change channels on the radio and television when violence, immoral behavior, and crude language are used. It will mean canceling some of our magazine subscriptions and refusing to continue reading certain books. It may mean refusing to frequent certain restaurants and internet sites. It does mean refusing to subject our hearts to a constant barrage of negative friends, words, thoughts, and conversations. It's bringing thoughts captive and choosing to focus on God and His attributes.

We need to fall on our knees daily and ask the Lord to remove heart attitudes not pleasing to Him. We need to be strong, courageous, and determined to yield our hearts to the Lord. Our attitudes should be, "Even though I don't want to do this, because I love You, I chose to trust You to give me the right heart attitude as I obey You." If we wait until we feel like doing something, we'll never do it. We must learn, as Mary did, to *willingly* obey…and not complain.

> And as we humbly bow before Him,
>   yielded with hearts open to Him,
>   He'll erase our regrets
>   and *wipe away our tears*.

Conclusion

PRESSING ON

Brethren, I count not myself to have apprehended:
but this one thing I do, forgetting those things which are
behind, and reaching forth unto those things which are before,
I press toward the mark for the prize of the high calling of God
in Christ Jesus.

Philippians 3:13-14

Passionately, Peter proclaimed the Gospel story of Christ's death, burial, resurrection, and ascension. Mary sat at the edge of the group between Joanna and Susanna listening to Peter and noting the people's response. Occasionally, she nudged Joanna and shook her head in agreement. They had heard news of the power of his preaching since Pentecost. Enticingly, he wooed them, speaking only the truth. His earnestness and humbleness gave credence to his words. It didn't matter that he wasn't an eloquent speaker and simply a fisherman. The people listened intently. Mary knew their hearts were softening to the truth.

She marveled at the change in Peter's life. This mighty man of God was her old friend. Yet she now saw no evidence of impulsiveness, impatience, or a short temper. He spoke with compassion and depth of understanding. His face even seemed to glow with love. Joy filled Mary's heart as she contemplated the progression of his transformed life.

Later that afternoon, after the crowd had left, Peter, Mary, Joanna, and Susanna sat together reminiscing and sharing events of their lives today. Not one of them had gone home and lived their lives as they had before they followed Jesus. They were different—changed. Life now had meaning and purpose. They wanted to share their discoveries about Christ with everyone they met. Excitedly, they shared instance after instance—with friends, children, men, women, shopkeepers, and families—when they had shared their testimonies.

Yes, there were heartaches and sometimes persecutions. But their desire to share with others the joy they had received from giving their hearts to the Lord, kept them faithfully persevering. They had no lingering thought about themselves, but sacrificially yielded their lives to be used in furthering the good news of Jesus Christ. Each was determined to press on. They remembered His love, and it compelled them to go on.

Finally, it was time to return home. The women must go their separate ways. Peter was drawn to other mission trips. Tenderly, they said their farewells, hating to leave the comfort and encouragement of being with fellow followers of Christ. At the same time, they were confident of meeting again someday...if not on earth, then in heaven.

❧ *Perhaps this was their final meeting.* ❧

Can't you just imagine the excitement of this group? It must have been electric, stimulating, and inspiring. I can see them waving to each other as they walked away energized and encouraged to continue sharing about Jesus.

Mary, the first to see the risen Lord and commissioned by Him to tell the disciples of this event, knew she must not disobey. She knew from experience how the Lord could take a miserable sinner and change them into something beautiful. She had to tell others of Jesus. It didn't matter if she felt inadequate, weary, or intimidated because she was a woman. There were no excuses where Christ was concerned. She had learned God likes to use the weak things of the world to confound the mighty, and the foolish to confound the wise. It pleased Him because He then received all the glory. She resolved that with His strength she could continue!

She echoed Isaiah's prayer, "Here I am, Lord. Use me."

Have you ever prayed that prayer?

Are you willing to be used?

Are you available?

Have you erased all the excuses you might use to keep from being obedient to His command to "go and tell"?

I believe Mary could confidently surrender because she knew how to abide in Christ. From the moment she met Him, she yearned to know more of Jesus. Any Pharisee or Sadducee could have made a fool of her doctrinally, but they could not discredit the fact that Jesus had cast out seven demons from her. She'd experienced His forgiveness and cleansing. Nothing could diminish the truth and the blessing of knowing the Lord.

The bearing of His message then was a light and easy yoke, for she spoke of what she knew and testified of what she had seen. She learned that sharing about the Lord was the easy part. The labor, the trials, the patience, the persistence, and the faith-stretching moments were in seeking and finding Jesus. And so it is with you and me. It's easier to share something we know and are passionate about.

The difficult part is choosing to know Him intimately. While we may desire to develop an intimate relationship with Him, usually we don't want to spend the time it takes growing the bond. Schedules, agendas, responsibilities, traffic, and families vie for our attention. Time after time we succumb to the world's pressures and postpone taking the necessary steps to nurture a mature relationship with the Lord and develop the transformed life.

It's a choice.

It's self-denial.

It's not easy, but it's worth it!

Does your relationship with Him cost you anything? What are you sacrificing to maintain an intimate relationship with the Lord? In Mary's case, it took self-denial to leave her home, family, and everything familiar to follow the Teacher. It took self-denial daily to continue living the nomadic life as she followed Him during His earthly ministry. And it took self-denial to tear herself away from the resurrected Lord and carry His message to the disciples.

Another word for *self-denial* is *surrender*. Lots of people make an impression. Surrendered people make an impact. Perhaps in the past, you've hesitated to surrender every area of your life into His control. You may consider yourself a slow starter. So was Peter. But he made a choice, and he learned it's not how you start but how you finish that counts.

Have you made that choice?

The Lord's message to Mary is the same for you and me and all those who believe on His name.

"Go and tell!"

What will your response be? You'll never hear His word without making a response—either negative or positive. You can't sit on the fence where God is concerned. With each of your responses, God will reply to you according to your answers to Him.

A transformed life is possible. It begins when you meet Jesus. It continues as you seek Him. And as surely as Jesus met Mary of Magdala and began her metamorphosis, He'll do the same for us. As she beheld the resurrected Lord, so shall we when we enter Heaven. What a meeting it will be!

> "And *God shall wipe away all tears from their eyes*; and there shall be no more death, neither sorrow, nor crying, neither shall there be any more pain: for the former things are passed away." (Revelation 21:4).

Until that time, press on! Refuse to give up! Find a way! Remember the woman with the issue of blood and the woman begging the unjust judge until he relented? They wouldn't give up. Be like Zacchaeus, though too short to see Jesus, he found a way—up a tree!

Press on when you're tired.

Press on when you don't understand.

Press on even when you have to go alone.

Press on toward the mark for the prize of the high calling of God in Christ Jesus.

Press on, precious one, He promises to...

Wipe Away All Our Tears!

NOT COMMITMENT, BUT SURRENDER

Am I serious about my relationship with You, Lord?
Am I willing to make changes even though they may be hard?
Do I really want my life to count for eternity?
Or am I just playing a game for others to see?

Oh, Lord, change me!
I choose to yield my life to Thee
for You gave Your life a ransom for me.

With each new day sweep clean the corners of my heart.
Help me to stand firm choosing from sin to depart.
Cover my mind with the blood of Your dear Son.
Help me to share with others that You are the Only One!

Oh, Lord, change me!
I choose to yield my life to Thee.
Mold me into a child that pleases Thee.

Keep me alert as I walk through my day
For the traps the enemy tries to lay.
May I see sin from Your point of view
Always choosing that which pleases You.

Oh, Lord, change me!
I choose to yield my life to Thee.
Cleanse me that I might spotless be.

Control my attitudes, mouth, and actions, Lord.
Empower me to change even though it will be hard.
Fill my life with joy that only comes from You.
May this not be a game, but a life that is true.

Oh, Lord, change me!
I choose to yield my life to Thee.
No longer me, but Thee may they see.

Edwina Patterson

About The Author

Edwina Patterson is a devoted wife and mother who is using her God-given talents and drawing upon her daily walk with Christ to write, teach, and speak to women who are seeking a deeper relationship with Him. She has ministered to literally thousands of women across the globe in churches and conferences for over thirty years. God has given her a heart for young married women and a sincere desire to help them develop an intimate relationship with the Lord through the foundation of prayer and Bible study.

Edwina is the founder of the non-profit organization, A Heart for the Home Ministry, as well as host of her original devotionals heard daily on local radio stations. She is a popular conference, retreat, and workshop speaker.

Edwina and R.J. Patterson have been married 41 years and make their home in Plano, Texas. They have three grown children and seven grandchildren.

For more information, please check her website:

www.heart-for-home.org

or call 1-800-344-8022.

Other Books by Edwina Patterson

REDEEMING THE TIME – WHERE DO I BEGIN?

REDEEMING THE TIME BIBLE STUDY

REDEEMING THE TIME WITH MY HUSBAND

REDEEMING THE TIME WITH MY CHILDREN

GOTTA MINUTE?

THAT I MIGHT NOT BE ASHAMED

PRAISE PRAYING FROM THE PSALMS

PRAISE PRAYING FROM THE PSALMS FOR CHILDREN

CHILDREN WHO GLORIFY GOD

GOD HAS BIG EARS … HE HEARS ME WHEN I PRAY

SHINING IN THE DARKNESS

IN A NUTSHELL

LISTENING FOR HIS VOICE